HOPE FOR THE MILLENNIUM

Also by David Pawson

Jesus Baptises in One Holy Spirit
The Normal Christian Birth
Once Saved, Always Saved?
The Road to Hell
Truth to Tell
When Jesus Returns
Word and Spirit Together

Hope for the Millennium

The Christian Debate About the Future

David Pawson

Hodder & Stoughton

LONDON SYDNEY AUCKLAND

Copyright © 1995, 1999 by David Pawson

First published as part of *When Jesus Returns*
in Great Britain 1995
This edition 1999

The right of David Pawson to be identified as the Author
of this Work has been asserted by him in accordance with the
Copyright, Designs and Patents Act 1988.

10 9 8 7 6 5 4 3 2 1

British Library Cataloguing in Publication Data
A record for this book is
available from the British Library

ISBN 0 340 73559 7

Typeset by Hewer Text Ltd, Edinburgh
Printed and bound in Great Britain by
Mackays of Chatham PLC, Chatham, Kent

Hodder and Stoughton Ltd
A Division of Hodder Headline PLC
338 Euston Road
London NW1 3BH

Contents

Introduction

God will not be celebrating the millennium.

The first day of January in the year 2000, or 2001 for that matter, is not a special date in his diary.

It is not the two thousandth birthday of his Son. Western civilisation uses the Gregorian calendar, named after the pope that inaugurated it. But it is at least a few years in error. Herod the Great, who slaughtered the baby boys in Bethlehem in the hope of exterminating Jesus, died in 4 BC.

So the date has no particular theological significance. But the 'millennium' has got spiritual connotations, especially for Christians and even for Jews, although for them 2000 will be the year 5760, the millennial year 6000.

There has been an extraordinary reversal in the use of the word itself. Centuries ago it was commonly heard inside the church, but rarely mentioned in the world outside. Today it is constantly spoken and written in society at large, but hardly ever in Christian pulpits or publications.

That is because its 'secular' meaning is universally under-stood and agreed: it refers to the advent of the year 2000. This is hailed as an excuse for extravagant celebrations, presumably because we have survived thus far! The fact that it is an approximate anniversary of the birth of Jesus is largely ignored, perhaps because it was too long ago to be of any contemporary relevance or significance.

The 'sacred' meaning linked the word with the second

advent of Jesus, not the first. It referred to the thousand years of peace and plenty that will follow his return to planet earth.

Alas, Christian opinions about this are now so confused and convictions so divided that there is an unspoken agreement not to talk about the subject at all, lest the fragile unity of Christians, particularly those calling themselves 'evangelicals' and believing the whole Bible to be the Word and words of God, be further imperilled.

The resulting silence is often justified by relegating millennial beliefs to a category of 'secondary' doctrines which are 'not necessary to salvation', along with other issues on which Christians disagree (like baptism). But since when have we been at liberty to decide which parts of God's revelation are essential to an understanding of his redemptive purpose and which are optional? Does not this kind of analysis imply a very limited scope of God's action in Christ, as if he only came to save individuals from hell? Why then did he teach his disciples to pray that the kingdom would come on earth as it is in heaven? Or promise that the meek would inherit the earth?

There are two tragic consequences of our general unwillingness to re-open the question, much less reach any conclusion firm enough to proclaim with confidence.

On the one hand, we are missing a glorious opportunity. With the word itself back in use, we could be using it as a starting-point for our good news. As so many others look forward to *their* millennium, we could be telling them how much more we are looking forward to *ours*. And we can give reasons for the hope that is in us. A better world is certainly coming, because Jesus is returning to reign.

Sadly, the Christian events planned for the year 2000 seem to major on the past, reminding those who will attend that the calendar marks the birth of Jesus two millennia ago.

But that will have been celebrated just ten days earlier, on 25 December 1999. Surely we ought to be looking forward rather than backward.

So, on the other hand, we are failing in a vital respon sibility. Followers of Jesus should be offering hope to the world, as well as faith and love. And hope is more needed as we reach the end of the twentieth century than it was at the beginning. Then, the word on everyone's lips was 'progress'.

The loss of the *Titanic* was the first major disaster to puncture that optimistic mood. It was the largest and most luxurious moving object man had ever made. With it sank the pride and confidence in human achievement. Two world wars followed, including the horror of genocide in the Holocaust. Proliferation of nuclear weapons and pollution of natural resources have left many uncertain of the future. Pessimism is widespread. The in-word is now 'survival'.

Like 'millennium', the word 'hope' has two different meanings. The world uses it about dreams which are un-certain ('I hope the weather will be good for our holiday', 'I hope I win the National Lottery', 'I hope the operation will cure it'). The New Testament uses it of events which are absolutely certain.

Few realise how accurate biblical predictions have proved to be. Altogether there are 735 separate forecasts of the future, of which 596 (81 per cent) have already come true, fulfilled quite literally. Less than 20 more need to happen before Jesus gets back – and his return is referred to 318 times. Impressive statistics, aren't they?

There are clear indications in scripture of where, how and even when we can expect him. But the supreme interest ought to be in the question why. What does he intend to do? How long will he need to stay on his second visit to achieve this? I have tackled these and many other issues in my book

When Jesus Returns (Hodder & Stoughton, 1995). This publication is actually the fourth section of that volume. The publishers suggested that it would make a useful contribution to Christian debate and witness as we draw near to the third millennium AD.

But the new millennium could well overlap with the *final* millennium of world history, which will be the best ever. There *is* hope for the world. It is hope for *the* millennium – not the next, but the last. And even that will not be the end, but the precursor of a completely recycled universe, including a brand new earth.

I have recently seized every chance I can to share such good news. At a recent tent mission in Windermere, I devoted one evening to this exciting topic. The reaction of a recently converted businessman was: 'Wow! This is big.' He had found the Lord Jesus Christ as his personal Saviour, but this was the first time he had heard that he was also the coming king of the whole world.

Those who believe this have been using a simple but sincere prayer for two thousand years:

'Even so, come, Lord Jesus; Amen.'

David Pawson

CHAPTER ONE

The Common Disappointment

The world is generally disappointed with Jesus. He has failed to live up to the expectations of Jew and Gentile alike.

JEWS

were the first to feel he had let them down. When he came, many were looking for the 'kingdom' or 'rule' of God to be re-established on planet earth. They believed he would send an 'anointed' king (in Hebrew: *meschiah*), of the Davidic dynasty, to accomplish this, through his chosen people, Israel. Their hopes, therefore, had both a national and international flavour.

On the one hand, their restored monarchy would bring the political freedom they had lost five centuries before and only briefly regained in the abortive Maccabean revolt against the Greeks. Now under Roman domination the longing for liberty continued, expressed in such phrases as 'the consolation of Israel' and 'the redemption of Jerusalem' (Luke 2:25,38).

On the other hand, they expected this liberation from other nations to give them a position of leadership to other nations, the 'tail' becoming the 'head' (Deut 28:13). Jerusalem would not just be their own capital; it would be the centre of world government (Mic 4:1–5; Isa 2:1–5). The just arbitration available in Zion would provide the proper basis for peace, leading to multilateral disarmament.

This dual dream, of national liberty and international leadership, is particularly clear in the later prophecies of Isaiah (note the interaction between 'Jerusalem' and 'nations/islands/ends of the earth' in chs. 40–66). It is typified in the words of the elderly Simeon when he caught sight of the baby Jesus in the temple courts – he told the Lord he could die happy, having seen 'a light for revelation to the Gentiles and for glory to your people Israel' (Luke 2:32).

Thirty-three years later Jesus left this earth without having accomplished either objective. Between his resurrection and ascension, the disappointed national aspiration was expressed more than once. 'We had hoped that he was the one who was going to redeem Israel' was the heartfelt cry of the two on the road to Emmaus (Luke 24:21). The very last question of the disciples was: 'Lord, are you at this time going to restore the kingdom [i.e. the monarchy] to Israel?' (Acts 1:6 – note that Jesus accepted the premises of the question, but told them the date set for that by 'the Father' was not their business).

It seems that Jesus himself had switched the focus of the kingdom from the national to the international dimension during his last six weeks on earth (Matt 28:19; Mark 16:15; Luke 24:47; Acts 1:3). Even earlier, he had announced that 'the kingdom of God will be taken away from you [i.e. Israel] and given to a people who will produce its fruit' (Matt 21:43).

This was not, as many have supposed, the cancellation of the national aspect. Too many scriptures point to a future place for Israel and Jerusalem in God's purposes to allow this conclusion (e.g. Matt 23:39; Luke 21:24; 22:29–30; Rom 11:1,11). Their part has been postponed. The order of events has been reversed. The Gentiles will receive the kingdom before the Jews (Rom 11:25–26). The first shall be last and the last first.

But has the rule of God been established among the nations, in accordance with this change of plan?

GENTILES

too, have expressed disillusionment with Jesus. It is commonly said that Christianity has been around for nearly *two thousand* years, yet the world is no better. If anything, it appears to be getting worse! The twentieth century has seen two major wars and the 'holocaust' in the 'civilised' continent of Europe. Evil seems more rampant and entrenched than ever. Yet over one third of the world's population carry the label 'Christian'.

Of course, we can say that many of the latter are only 'nominal' in their religious allegiance. Or we can claim with G.K. Chesterton that 'the Christian ideal has not been tried and found wanting; it has been found difficult and left untried'. And we could make quite a list of benefits to mankind which have sprung from Christian compassion – the emancipation of slaves and women, the care of sick and handicapped, orphaned and illiterate. A strong case can be made for the Christian origins of modern science and all its achievements.

Yet the criticism can still be made. Few would boldly claim that the world is now a safer, happier, better place to live in. Fewer still would claim that this is largely due to the influence of Christ. The New Testament assessment that 'the whole world is under the control of the evil one' (1 John 5:19) seems as accurate now as it was then.

CHRISTIANS

also have their doubts. A large proportion seem to have accepted that this world will never be any different. Their hope for the future is centred on the next world. Their task is seen as the saving of as many individuals as possible from a society that is terminally sick.

Surprisingly, and perhaps in reaction to such pessimism, there is another sector of the Christian spectrum which has confidence to think that the church is well on the way to taking over national and international governments. Christians could become the majority and therefore play a decisive role in social, political and universal affairs.

Perhaps most believers are in between these two extremes, seeking realism rather than gloomy pessimism or naive optimism. In addition to evangelising, they believe they must be doing whatever they can to make this world better by working for the welfare of both individuals and communities.

Not all of these will ask about the ultimate goal of their endeavours. Many will be content with meeting some immediate needs. Even if the total scene gets worse, they will be satisfied that they have 'done their bit'. That is infinitely preferable to being so depressed about the whole trend that action is paralysed.

But the question of ultimate outcome cannot be shelved. Faith and love are not sufficient to sustain full Christian service. Hope is the vital third dimension. It is 'an anchor for the soul' (Heb 6:19), especially when experiencing discouragement and the temptation to despair. The thought of final success gives the strength to overcome all intermediate obstacles.

Jesus taught his followers to pray every day that the

kingdom of God, the divine rule, would 'come on earth . . . as it is in heaven' (Matt 6:10). Clearly, this has not happened yet or we would not need to go on using this petition. But what are we praying for? What do we expect to happen when the prayer is answered? Someone has said that our whole theology can be deduced from our answers to these questions!

Will the kingdom come on earth? If so, how and when? Will it come gradually or suddenly? By human infiltration or divine intervention? Will it be purely spiritual or political as well?

To put it another way, will the Lord Jesus Christ ever rule this world in such a visible way that everyone knows that all authority has been given to him in heaven and on earth (Matt 28:18), that he is the King of kings and Lord of lords (Rev 19:16), that every knee must bow to him and every tongue confess his lordship (Phil 2:11)? Or will only Christians 'see' these things by faith?

We are already discussing the issue of 'the millennium'! For these are the very questions that lie at the heart of the debate.

Far too many dismiss the subject as an academic debate with little or no practical significance. What is the point of arguing over the interpretation of 'one obscure passage in a highly symbolic book'? The resulting differences are said to threaten the unity of the church and distract it from its mission.

But we have already seen that future expectations are the essence of the Christian virtue of hope. We are saved by faith and in hope (Rom 8:24).

Let it be stated at once that there is widespread agreement about the *next* world, that 'new heaven and new earth' (Rev 21:1) that will succeed this old universe, though it is usually referred to as 'heaven', with little or no emphasis on 'earth'.

There are few arguments about the last two chapters in the Bible!

The real differences emerge when the future hopes for *this* world are discussed. How far will the divine authority given to Jesus be made manifest in this world before it comes to an end? As we have already indicated, there is a huge range of Christian opinion, which has grown wider over the centuries of church history.

The controversy, fierce at times, has centred on the twentieth chapter of the book of Revelation. This is hardly surprising, since it appears to cover the very last events of this age, leading up to the final day of judgement, which in turn ushers in the new creation.

From this chapter a simple reader could easily conclude that Christ and his followers, particularly those who have been martyred for their faith, will actually 'reign' over this world for one thousand years before it comes to an end.

It is from this repeated phrase 'a thousand years' that the word *millennium* has come (from the Latin: *mille* = thousand and *annum* = year). Hence the noun 'millennialism' describes the belief that Christ will reign on earth for this period. The doctrine is sometimes called 'chiliasm' (in Greek: *chilioi* = thousand).

As we approach the end of the twentieth century the word 'millennium' has come back into daily use, since on 1 January 2001, we shall enter the third millennium AD (Latin for *anno domini* = year of our Lord). This date on the calendar has led directly to renewed interest in the promised return of our Lord and indirectly to renewed debate about his 'millennial' reign on earth, especially among those who still believe the twenty-first century will begin the seventh millennium since creation (a kind of cosmic 'sabbath'), by assuming creation took place in 4004 BC, as a note in some old Bibles suggested.

We must not let dating attempts obscure the real issue by bringing the debate into speculative disrepute. The primary question is not when but whether. Will Christ ever rule this world for a thousand years?

Our starting point must obviously be the passage of scripture from which many have reached a positive conclusion, namely, Revelation 20. This will be studied in detail and in context. Then we shall work backwards through the New and Old Testaments to see if we find confirmation or contradiction of our findings. After that we shall work forwards through church history, noting when and why very different interpretations arose. These will be assessed for their exegetical accuracy and practical influence. Finally, I will give the reasons for my own conclusion and conviction.

The current position is much more complex than many realise. Most readers will probably be familiar with the three labels: a-millennial, pre-millennial and post-millennial. A friend of mine, when asked which described his own view, replied: 'That is *a pre-post*-erous question!' Others avoid committing themselves by saying they are pan-millennial, explaining the prefix to mean that 'things will pan out alright in the end whatever we think now'!

However, jocular evasions cannot diminish the importance of reaching some conclusion. As we shall see, our real belief will have a profound effect on our attitude to this world and our responsibility for it. So we need to be clear.

One problem is that each of the three main approaches has two quite different variations, so that in reality there are six positions from which to choose. A further complication is that most who call themselves 'a-millennial' are actually one subdivision of 'post-millennial', though this is rarely realised. Keep reading and all will be made clear!

Meanwhile, it is with some relief that we turn to scripture

itself and begin our study by looking at what the Bible actually *says* before we consider what others think it *means*. As we do so, we constantly need to recall that the book of Revelation was written for ordinary believers in the seven churches of Asia (now western Turkey). It was not a complex conundrum for theological professors and biblical scholars to unravel. It is a sound principle to read scripture in its plain, simple sense unless there is a clear indication that it should be taken otherwise. We must seek to recover the message it would communicate to its original readers.

With these few guidelines we can now approach the key passage, over which there has been so much debate.

CHAPTER TWO

The Basic Passage (Revelation 20)

This is undoubtedly the clearest passage on the 'millennium' in the whole Bible. Some would say it is the only passage about it. Certainly, without this chapter it would not be an issue. Life would be much simpler if it wasn't there at all! Those who wish that were so and try to ignore it need to be reminded of the curse on those who take anything away from 'this prophecy' (Rev 22:19); they could lose their place in eternity!

Those who believe that the Bible consists of, and not just contains, the inspired words of God must take this chapter seriously. Even if it were the only mention of this part of his purpose, it would still be his Word. How often does God have to say something before we believe it?

So we must let the passage speak for itself. But first we must see it in its context – not just its immediate context (chapters 19 and 21) but its wider setting.

It is in the New Testament, not the Old. It belongs to the 'new' covenant of Jesus, not the 'old' covenant of Moses. It is addressed to Christians rather than Jews. Though 'Jewish' in atmosphere (the book of Revelation contains four hundred allusions to Hebrew scriptures, though not a single quotation), it is intended for Gentile believers and does not need to be re-interpreted for them (as would the Deuteronomic laws, for example). This is written by a Christian for Christians.

This chapter is part of a unique book in the New Testament. In another section of *When Jesus Returns* we examined Revelation in greater detail (see pages 85–172); but a brief summary is needed here.

It is basically a letter, a composite circular epistle to a group of churches – but here all similarity (e.g. to Ephesians) ends. It was never intended to be written! It is a transcription of verbal and visual reflections which came unexpectedly to a man in prison who was told by an angel to write them down and pass them on. This is probably why the letter is described as a 'prophecy', the only such in the New Testament. It is both a word for the present (forthtelling) and about the future (foretelling), with the major emphasis on the latter. Nearly two thirds of its 'verses' contain predictions, covering fifty-six separate events. Inevitably, pictorial language is used to describe the unknown and even unimaginable; but the symbolism is intended to clarify rather than conceal and is rarely obscure.

The book/prophecy/letter is intended to be read aloud (note the blessing on reader and hearers in Rev 1:3). Perhaps it is only in these circumstances that it yields its deepest meaning and makes its greatest impact.

Above all, we need constantly to remember that its purpose is intensely practical: to prepare Christian individuals and churches for tougher times ahead. Its aim is to encourage (to put courage into) believers to 'endure' suffering for their faith even to the point of martyrdom, and to 'overcome' all hostile pressures, thus keeping their names in the 'book of life' (Rev 3:5;14:12). Every part of the book is directed to this end. Of each passage and its interpretation the question must be asked: how does this help persecuted disciples?

The book divides into clear sections. The most obvious division is between the first three chapters, which deal with the readers' *present* situation, and the remainder, which unveils the *future* to them (see 4:1). The latter section goes right to the end of the world and beyond, but divides into two phases, which may be seen as 'bad news' and 'good news'. This simple threefold message may be presented as follows:

i. Things which must be put right now (1–8).
ii. Things will get much worse before they get better (4–18).
iii. Things will get much better after they get worse (19–22).

The second section deals with the more immediate future while the third deals with the ultimate future, with the very last things. It is the return of Christ to planet earth which turns the tide in the flow of events (Rev 19:11–16).

Chapter 20 sits firmly in this third section. It belongs to the 'last things'. It is part of the 'good news'. It is part of that encouraging future to which the persecuted can look forward and for which they should be willing to die.

At this point it is necessary to introduce an important principle of biblical study: namely, to *ignore chapter divisions*! They were not in the original text. Though convenient for reference, they are not inspired by God and are often in the wrong place, putting asunder what God has joined together! The large figure '20' is seriously misleading (another argument for reading the book aloud). The continuity clearly apparent in the original is violently disrupted and this has enabled commentators to separate the chapter from its context, radically to revise its message and application and to relocate the millennium in history (more of that later).

When the chapter divisions are ignored and 'chapters'

18-22 are read as a continuous narrative, a remarkable pattern emerges. It could be entitled: 'A tale of two cities' (Babylon and Jerusalem) which are personified as two women, a filthy prostitute and a pure bride. The destruction of the one metropolis and the descent of the other are separated by an extraordinary series of events, revealed in a sevenfold vision.

It is instructive to note the switches from verbal to visual revelations. The fall of Babylon is told by an angel and is 'heard' by John (18:4), as is the heavenly rejoicing over it (19:1,6). John is then told to write down what he has *heard* (19:9). After these voices comes a series of visions, which John *saw* (19:11, 17, 19; 20:1, 4, 11; 21:1). Seven things are 'seen' before the next thing is 'heard' (21:3). This series of visions may be listed as follows:

1. The rider on a white horse at the open door of heaven.
2. An angel invites birds to the 'last supper' of human flesh.
3. The battle with all anti-God forces at Armageddon.
4. An angel binds, banishes and imprisons the devil.
5. The saints reign with Christ for a thousand years, at the end of which Satan is released, defeated and thrown into the lake of fire.
6. The resurrection of the dead and the final day of judgement.
7. The creation of a new heaven and a new earth; and the descent of the new Jerusalem.

Seven is, of course, a familiar number in this book, beginning with the seven churches of Asia and the seven letters to them. More significant are the three series of disasters under the figure of seals, trumpets and bowls.

The latter clearly present a sequence of events, increasing in intensity. Furthermore, in each series the first four belong together (the clearest example is the four horsemen of the first four seals in 6:1–8), the next two are related and the last or seventh stands on its own. The same 4–2–1 pattern may be clearly discerned in the final series of visions we are now examining (in 19:11 to 21:2).

Once the chapter numbers (20 and 21) have been removed, the series of seven visions clearly presents a sequence of events, each relating to the preceding one. There is internal evidence that the visions are consecutive, in chronological order. Two examples will suffice:

i.   The devil is thrown into the lake of fire *after* the beast and the false prophet (compare 20:10 with 19:20).
ii. The new heaven and earth appear *after* the old have passed away (compare 21:1 with 20:11).

In particular, to separate chapter 20 from chapter 19 destroys the whole sequence. This is widely done in the interests of the a-millennial and post-millennial positions, who want to make chapter 20 a 'recapitulation' of the whole church age and not a sequel to the events of chapter 19. This should be seen as an artificial separation, relying heavily on the medieval chapter divisions.

The sequence belongs together. The only valid question is: what period of time does it cover?

All agree on when it *ends*. The day of judgement (vision 6) and the new heaven and earth (vision 7) take us to the very end of this age, what we know as 'history'.

But when does it *begin*? Who is the rider on the white horse and when does he come charging with the forces of heaven?

There is no argument about his identity. The titles 'Faithful and True' (applied to Jesus in 3:14); 'Word of God' (only used elsewhere in the New Testament of Jesus in John 1:1,14) and 'King of kings and Lord of lords' (identified with 'the Lamb' in 17:14) leave no room for doubt. He is the Lord Jesus Christ. (Note that this is not necessarily the case in 6:2, where the rider is not identified, uses a bow rather than a sword and the emphasis is on the colour of the horse – a general symbol of military aggression.)

There is some disagreement about his 'exit' from heaven. The choice is between his first and second advent.

The small number of scholars who claim this to be a representation of his *first* visit to earth do so in order to retain the sevenfold sequence while applying the 'millennium' to the church age. To maintain this, the details have to be heavily 'allegorised'. The white horse of conquest is a purely 'spiritual' symbol, for in actuality he rode on a donkey of peace (Matt 21:4–5, fulfilling Zech 9:9). The stained robe is only his own blood. The striking down of the nations is only metaphorical, though of what is not usually stated. But this whole attempt to maintain the sequence fails because it involves applying the decisive battle of 'Armaggedon' to the crucifixion, which means that the beast and the false prophet were 'thrown alive into the fiery lake' at Calvary! This makes nonsense of their appearance in chapter 13 among the things that 'must take place after this' (4:1). This approach creates more problems than it solves and has convinced very few.

Most are agreed that the first vision (19:11–16) refers to the *second* advent of Christ. There are many sound reasons for this conclusion. First, this 'warlike' mission is far more compatible with his second coming 'to judge the living and the dead'. Second, the enemies he destroys here are human as well as demonic, which was not the case at his first coming. Third, the preceding context is the announcement of a wedding and a 'ready' bride, which naturally leads into the coming of the Bridegroom (compare Matt 25:6). Fourth, and this seems decisive, if this is not a reference to the second advent then our Lord's return is nowhere mentioned in the main body of this prophecy, though both the prologue and epilogue indicate it as the main theme (1:7 and 22:20). It is hardly surprising that most commentaries accept this interpretation. The sequence begins at the second advent.

We may pick out four major events in the sevenfold vision:

1. The second advent (ch. 19)
2. The millennial reign (ch. 20)
3. The judgement day (ch. 20)
4. The new creation (ch. 21)

Almost all biblical scholars accept 1, 3 and 4 events as belonging to the end of history and in that same order! But there is a widespread reluctance to include 2 in the sequence, though it clearly belongs there. This is due in turn to a long-standing tradition in the church which has rejected so-called 'pre-millennialism' (the belief that 1 precedes 2 in time, that Jesus returns before he and his saints reign). This has resulted in extraordinary attempts to prove that Revelation 19–21 really intends the reader to understand the order of events as 2, 1, 3, 4 – in spite of the pattern in which they are there presented!

This subtle juxtaposition is not based on any clear indication in the text itself. It results from bringing to the text a prior conviction (the exact meaning of 'prejudice'), in this case the assumption that nothing intervenes between the return of Christ and the day of judgement. This has been the majority opinion in the church for many centuries and has been implied in its creeds (both the Apostles' and the Nicene). Christ was thought of as coming again to judge rather than to reign.

There are some scriptures which seem to uphold this compression of events and we shall look at them later. It is often claimed that they are 'plain' statements, whereas Revelation 20 is said to be 'obscure'. Having made this judgement, it is then argued that the latter should be interpreted in the light of the former – which usually means forcing the one to fit the other.

Even if it were 'obscure', that is no reason to dismiss it. Some seem to think that to say it is 'highly symbolic' excuses them from taking it seriously or even explaining what are the realities behind the symbols. And they seem ready enough to take the first and last visions at face value!

But is it so obscure? There seems to this writer very limited use of symbolic language in these visions. Most of the events are stated as fact, actual occurrences. The figures of speech are hardly mysterious: 'four corners of the earth' is perfectly obvious and need not be taken to mean the writer believed the earth was square. Who doesn't understand what 'the great white throne' stands for? The only really puzzling reference is to 'Gog and Magog', but a glance at Ezekiel 39 suggests them to be labels for the last prince and people to attack God's people *after* David's dynasty has been restored.

The time has come to study the passage (20:1–10) in detail, allowing the text to speak for itself before comparing it with other relevant scriptures. We shall seek to study it with the reverence due to the inspired words of God and the integrity of an open mind concerned with objective exegesis.

The first thing to notice is the repeated use of the phrase 'thousand years' – six times in one short passage. In two of these the definite article makes it still more emphatic: '*the* thousand years'. It could hardly be more precise.

Some want to take it as a symbol, citing ten cubed as an indication of completeness. But even those who do so usually say it represents an extended period of *time*, as opposed to a brief interval. It is much more than an interlude. It is an epoch which has significance in its own right.

The case for taking the phrase literally rests on the fact that other spans of time are specifically denoted in this book. For example, the duration of the 'Great Tribulation', or 'Big Trouble', is said to last for 'a time, times and half a time' (12:14), or '1,260 days' (12:6) or 'forty-two months' (13:5).

The contrast between these three and a half years of intense suffering for the saints and the following thousand years of reigning with Christ is very much in line with the whole purpose of the book – to encourage faithfulness in the present by thought about the future. As Paul wrote: 'I consider that our present sufferings are not worth comparing with the glory that will be revealed in us' (Rom 8:18).

In further consideration of the ten 'verses' as a whole, we can ask the usual basic questions: when, where and who?

WHEN do 'the thousand years' occur? The twofold answer is clear from the 'sevenfold vision' of which they are a part: *after* the rider on the white horse (Jesus) has defeated the beast and the false prophet and *before* the great white throne. In other words, the millennium lies *between* the second advent and the day of judgement.

WHERE do Christ and his saints reign? In heaven or on earth? The book of Revelation keeps alternating between heaven and earth (4:1;7:1;8:1, etc.). But there is usually a very clear indication of location. So which is the setting for chapter 20?

We must begin with chapter 19. Heaven is 'open' for the rider (19:11), but it is then very obvious that he comes to earth for the battle with evil forces (19:19). The angel binding Satan comes 'down out of heaven' (20:1). His later release also takes place on 'earth' (20:8–9). The 'earth' later disappears before the final judgement (20:11).

The whole focus is on 'earth', throughout this passage. In the absence of any hint to the contrary, we may take the millennial reign of the saints to take place on this 'old' earth before it disappears. A sudden shift to heaven in verses 4–6 would have been clearly indicated. Furthermore, the saints reign 'with Christ' (20:4) and he has by now returned to earth (19:11–21).

The wider context of the whole book confirms this in three earlier announcements. Those who overcome will be given 'authority over the nations' (2:26). Those who are redeemed by the blood of the Lamb will 'reign on the earth' (5:10). The 'kingdom of the world' will become the kingdom of Christ (11:15). None of these promises is fulfilled until chapter 20.

WHO is the central figure in this passage? Surprisingly, it is not Christ! He is only mentioned incidentally. Most of the attention is on Satan, though his part in the millennium is limited to the very beginning and the very end. The saints are in the forefront during the centuries between. The structure of the passage is therefore a 'sandwich':

1–3   Satan removed (brief)
4–6   Saints reigning (lengthy)
7–10   Satan released (brief)

A reason must be found for this extraordinary disproportion of content. Meanwhile, we will consider each of the three 'paragraphs' in greater depth.

SATAN REMOVED (20:1–3)

To understand what is happening here, we need to look again at the wider context.

Four alien and hostile figures have already been introduced. Three are actual persons, two of them human: Satan (hurled to earth in ch. 12), the 'antichrist' and the false prophet (emerging in ch. 13). Together they form an 'unholy trinity', taking over world government at the climax of history, causing the greatest distress for the people of God. They are all male. The fourth is female, but is not a person. She, a prostitute, is a 'personification' – of a city, 'Babylon', the commercial hub of the world.

These four dominate the final but very brief period of this 'present evil age'. They are dealt with in reverse order to their appearance:

Babylon falls (ch. 18).
Antichrist and false prophet are thrown into hell, the first humans to go there (ch. 19).
Satan is removed, released, then thrown into hell himself (ch. 20).

It will be noted that Satan's doom is phased and includes an astonishing development (in 7–10).

Phase 1 is his removal from the earth. His two human puppets, the political dictator and his religious accomplice, have already been consigned to the 'fiery lake' (19:20). But that is not to be his fate – yet. He is to be confined rather than consigned, taken into custody to await final judgement (as some of his colleagues are already; 2 Pet 2:4; Jude 6).

Who will remove him? Not God, not Christ, not the church, but one unnamed angel. What an indignity for one who has had the whole world in his power (1 John 5:19)! This point is important, for this act has sometimes been confused with statements in the Gospels (e.g. Matt 12:29; 16:19).

How will he be removed? This has misleadingly been called 'the binding of Satan' by those who want to identify it with Jesus' victory over the devil when tempted in the wilderness (Luke 4:13–14; Matt 12:29). But it is far more than being bound. There are five verbs, not one. Satan is seized, chained, thrown, locked, sealed. He is thus rendered totally ineffective as well as removed altogether from his earthly sphere of influence. The incident should be labelled the *banishment* of Satan. The master of disguise and distortion is no longer around. He is unable to 'deceive the nations' any more (20:3).

To say that this has already happened is surely to be self-deceived. Yet this is frequently done in the interests of identifying the 'millennium' with the present church age. His 'binding' is then limited to failing to prevent the spread of the gospel, while unbelievers remain firmly under his control. The absurdity of this application is obvious. If the world is like it is after Satan has been seized, chained, thrown, locked and sealed, what will it be like when he is 'released' again?! Who would dare claim that he is not deceiving the nations right now?

Where will he be confined? Not on the earth, but 'under' it. The word used for his location (in Greek *abussos* = bottomless) refers to the immeasurable underworld, the lowest region of the abode of the dead, the home of demons (cf. Deut 30:13; Rom 10:7; Luke 8:31); it is used seven times in Revelation (9:1,2,11; 11:7; 17:8; 20:1, 3). Another name for this place of imprisonment is 'Tartarus' (this familiar term from the pagan world is used in 2 Pet 2:4). Wherever this is, it is certainly not *on* earth.

However, this incarceration is not permanent. God has one more purpose for Satan, which comes as a complete surprise later in this chapter. What happens in the meanwhile, between his restraint and subsequent release?

SAINTS REIGNING (20:4–6)

The removal of the beast, the false prophet (19:20) and the devil (20:3) will leave a political vacuum in the world. Who will take over its government? But a prior question needs to be faced: will there be a need for anyone to take it over? To put it another way: will there be anyone left to govern?

Will anyone survive the 'Armageddon' conflict described in chapter 19? First impressions might suggest that no one is left alive on earth. The vultures are invited to consume 'the flesh of all people' (19:18). After the two leaders are taken captive alive, the 'rest of them' are killed (19:21). This has been taken to refer to the entire population of the world, but a more careful reading shows that these inclusive terms are qualified by the term 'the kings of the earth and their armies', that is, the vast host that had 'gathered' for the battle (19:19).

That many people are not involved is clearly indicated in the sequel, where Satan has to be restrained from deceiving 'the nations' (20:3) and later is able to gather a huge following on his release (20:8).

So there will still be a need for world government. Who will constitute it? The answer is both individual and corporate: Christ and his faithful followers.

The word 'thrones' is plural (the only other such in the whole book is 4:4). Since the scene is on earth, they are not to be confused with either God's eternal throne in heaven (chs. 4–5) or with the 'great white throne' of final judgement after earth has 'fled' (20:11). The collective noun covers all 'seats of government', local, regional, national and international. Their purpose is the administration of justice; they will be used by those 'given authority to judge' (20:4). But who are they?

Here we face a rather difficult grammatical issue: does the text indicate one, two or three groups of 'rulers'? At first sight, it seems that only those who have been martyred for Christ reign with him. They have been 'beheaded because of their testimony for Jesus and because of the word of God' (20:4; this dual charge was the reason for John's imprisonment and the basis of his call for endurance, 1:9; 14:12). They have been 'faithful, even to the point of death' (2:10), which means to the extent of dying, not just until the moment of dying; it is widely misapplied at funerals after natural death.

Closer examination reveals that 'those given authority to judge' are not necessarily the same as those 'beheaded'. Note the extra phrase: '*and* I saw' inserted between the two groups. It sounds as if they are not entirely the same, yet not entirely different! The simplest explanation is that the latter is a section of the former. John sees the faithful followers of Jesus sharing his reign and particularly notices among them those who chose to die rather than deny their Lord. This would fit in with the promise that *all* who hold on until he comes and do his will 'to the end' will rule the nations (2:25–27), while for *some* this will mean martyrdom (2:10).

It is easy to see why the latter should be singled out for special mention. What an encouragement to those hearing the death sentence pronounced on them by earthly judges to know that one day they would be sitting on their 'thrones'. This would combine vindication with compensation. At a deeper level, their own experience of injustice in court would strengthen their ambition to be absolutely fair when they come to carry the responsibility. What an amazing reversal of roles!

Some have seen yet another subgroup in those who had 'not worshipped the beast or his image and had not received his mark on their foreheads or on their hands' (20:4). This could refer to those who refused to give in, but escaped with their lives. That there will be such is hinted at elsewhere in Revelation (12:6,17 and 18:4, for example). If there were no survivors, there would be no living saints to greet Christ on his return, to be 'changed in the twinkling of an eye' (1 Cor 15:51–52; 1 Thess 4:17). But whether Revelation 20 specifically refers to these or is further defining the 'beheaded' is an open question; this author inclines to the latter. The former would be included in the larger body first mentioned.

So one overall group is in view, with focus on one section in the fore-ground – saints in general and martyrs in particular.

How can martyrs be reigning on this earth? Put out of the world for their faith, they are now back in it. They must have been brought back to life, their disembodied spirits re-embodied for life here on earth. In other words they have experienced a 'resurrection' (20:15; this noun, *anastasis*, used 42 times in the New Testament, always refers to a physical miracle, the raising of a body; it is never used of regeneration, the new birth). The language implies that John actually saw this happening in his vision of the future, so the 'picture' was a movie! He had earlier seen the 'souls' of the martyrs crying for divine retribution on their murderers (6:9). Now he sees them in resurrected bodies reigning on the earth.

This is yet another clear indication that the millennial reign follows the second coming of Jesus, since it is at that moment that 'those who belong to him' receive their new bodies (1 Cor 15:23; 1 Thess 4:16).

The distinction between this 'first resurrection' of the 'blessed and holy' and 'the rest of the dead' could hardly be clearer. We know from other scriptures that the whole human race, the wicked as well as the righteous, will be raised from the dead before the day of judgement (Dan 12:2; John 5:29; Acts 24:15). However, to refer to this *fact* as 'the general resurrection', an unbiblical term, is misleading, since it implies a single *event*. In Revelation we learn that the two categories are raised on different dates, widely separated in time. There will be two resurrections, the 'first' and the 'rest', at the beginning and end of 'the thousand years'.

That the two happenings are identical in nature is confirmed by the use of exactly the same verb for both (the third person plural aorist tense indicative of *zao*, which means: to exercise the functions of life, here translated as 'come to life'). It is true that this word can very occasionally be used in a spiritual sense (e.g. John 5:25, where the context indicates this metaphorical use); but its normal meaning is physical (as in John 11:25; Rom 14:9), particularly in this book so far (Rev 1:18; 2:8; 13:14).

There is the further point that 'came to life' in verse 4 is in clear contrast to 'beheaded', both physical events. They must have been 'spiritually raised with Christ' long before their martyrdom; and after it they were fully conscious and able to communicate with him (6:9). Like him, they experienced physical death and resurrection – but neither interrupted their 'spiritual' or even 'mental' life, which was continuous from their conversion. It was their bodies that 'came to life', enabling them again to function in this physical world.

Without labouring the point, it is important to emphasise it, since both a-millennial and post-millennial viewpoints give the verb two entirely different meanings – spiritual regeneration in verse 4 and physical resurrection of the body in verse 5, though there is not a hint of this switch in the text itself. This violates an elementary rule of exegesis: the same word in the same context has the same meaning unless *clearly* indicated otherwise. Let an older scholar, Dean Alford, summarise this inconsistency:

> . . . if in such a passage the first resurrection may be understood to mean *spiritual* rising with Christ, while the second means *literal* rising from the grave; then there is an end to all significance in language, and Scripture is wiped out as a testimony to anything. If the first resurrection is spiritual, then so is the second, which I suppose none will be hardy enough to maintain; but if the second is literal, then so is the first, which in common with the whole primitive Church and many of the best modern expositors, I do maintain and receive as an article of faith and hope. (Quoted in William E. Biederwolf, *The Prophecy Handbook*, World Bible Publishers, 1991 reprint of 1924 original, p. 697)

This concept of two resurrections, of the righteous and the wicked, widely separated in time, was not original to this book. The idea was quite widespread among the Jews of Jesus' day. Many expected the 'righteous' dead to be raised before the Messianic reign on earth, while the wicked would only be raised for judgement at its end (some already said the interval between would be a thousand years). That is why Jesus could refer, without explanation, to 'the resurrection of the righteous', when talking to Pharisees (Luke 14:14). They already believed in two resurrections, while the Sadducees believed in none (Luke 20:27).

Three statements are made about those who 'have part' in

the first resurrection. First, their *sanctity*. They are 'blessed and holy'. By implication those in the second are cursed and evil. Second, their *security*. At the second coming their salvation from sin will be complete (Phil 1:6; 1 John 3:2). They will be sure then that there will be no further risk of suffering 'the second death' which is 'the lake of fire' (20:6,14). Third, their *sovereignty*. Their 'kingship' will be combined with priesthood (compare 1:6 with 20:6). They will act as managers for Christ and mediators for the people. This dual function replaces the political role of the beast and the religious role of the false prophet.

This situation is not permanent. The 'reign' on this earth will end with this earth, though it will continue in the new earth (22:5). The 'thousand years' come to an end in the most surprising manner:

SATAN RELEASED (20:7–10)

The development revealed here is so totally unexpected that it could hardly have been invented by human imagination. Its very strangeness is a hallmark of divine inspiration.

We now see why Satan was not thrown into hell earlier, along with his two human agents (19:20). God is going to use him just once more. He is to be given a final fling! Released on parole, he is allowed to 'deceive the nations' one last time.

The nature of this deception has much in common with his very first trickery of the human race (Gen 3). Then it was two persons, now it is many ethnic groups. But the appeal is the same: moral autonomy, freedom from God's government (which now includes Christ and his saints). Since this 'kingdom' is now on earth, a literal 'body', it can be attacked with military might. A huge force is gathered from 'the four corners of the earth' to march on the seat of government, 'the city he [God] loves', clearly Jerusalem, the millennial headquarters of the 'United Nations' (20:9; cf. Isa 2:1–5; Mic 4:1–5; Matt 5:35).

This last 'battle' of all must not be confused with 'Armageddon', which was only the sixth bowl (16:16) and took place before the thousand years (19:19–21). It is identified by a different title, 'Gog and Magog', the names used by Ezekiel for the 'prince' and his followers who attack the land of Israel *after* God's people are re-established there and the Davidic dynasty restored to the throne (see Ezek 37–39). It seems that 'Gog' in Revelation is the last of a number of names given to Satan (like 'Apollyon' in 9:11 and 'Beelzebub' in Matt 10:25) and 'Magog' refers to the international army he persuades to fight for him.

The attempt to besiege and attack the world capital fails completely. The battle is never joined. Neither Christians nor Christ himself need to engage the enemy. God himself sends 'fire from heaven' (Gen 15:17; Lev 9:24; Judg 13:20; 1 Kgs 18:38; 2 Chr 7:1; Luke 9:54; Rev 9:18). Though the devil could tap such destructive power (13:13), it is now used to destroy his entire militia. He himself is thrown into the lake of fire, where his two human agents have already been for the thousand years.

Verse 10 is very important. It is the clearest statement of the nature of hell in the New Testament. The language is plain and simple; it cannot be dismissed as 'highly symbolic'. It is a place of 'torment', which can mean nothing other than conscious pain, whether physical or emotional, or both. This understanding goes back to Jesus himself (Matt 25:30; Luke 16:23–25). The suffering is continuous ('day and night') and never-ending ('for ever and ever' is an English equivalent of the Greek phrase *eis tous aionas ton aionon*, literally 'into the ages of the ages', the very strongest phrase in that language for everlasting time, cf. 4:9–10; 5:13–14; 7:12; 10:6; 11:15; 14:11; 15:7; 19:3; 22:5).

Since 'they', the subject of this statement, includes two human beings, the modern notion of 'annihilationism' (the belief that the 'wicked' are consigned to oblivion by extinction, either at death or after the day of judgement) is quite ruled out. Jesus taught the same punishment for all he would reject in judgement (Matt 25:41, 46). For a fuller treatment of this vital issue, see my book: *The Road to Hell* (Hodder and Stoughton 1992).

So ends Satan's reign in this world. Having been the prince, ruler and even 'god' of this world (John 12:31; 2 Cor 4:4), he now meets his doom and shares the common destiny of all who rebel against the kingly rule of God, whether human or angelic (Matt 25:41; Rev 12:4).

Did he not expect this to happen? Did he expect his last bid for earthly sovereignty to succeed? Was he self-deluded as well as the deceiver of nations? Did he really think he was stronger than God's people and therefore than God himself? Or did he, knowing his fate was sealed and his end near, seek to take as many as he could to share his ruin, in a last fit of frustrated rage? Perhaps we shall never know. Perhaps we don't need to.

In fact, this whole passage raises many tantalising questions, to which no answers are given. Hardly anything is said about the 'millennium' itself and how it will be worked out in practice. We can only conclude that such information was not relevant to the purpose of Revelation. It is enough to know that the forces of good will be publicly vindicated and the forces of evil finally removed.

So we have the basic facts. We are told *what* will happen at the end, but not *why* events will take this course. Of course, God is not obliged to give us his reasons for anything he does, as Job found out the hard way many centuries ago (Job 40:1–5; 42:1–6). There is a place for reverent agnosticism (Rom 9:20).

Yet the conundrum persists. Why 'on earth' is the devil given a final chance to do such damage at the very end of a thousand years of good government? And why 'on earth' is there such a thousand years anyway? While avoiding sheer speculation, we may feel our way towards an understanding by considering the spiritual effects of these two developments.

To take the positive one first, the millennial rule of Christ and his saints on this earth will be a visible vindication of him and them in the eyes of the world. It will demonstrate just what this world can be like when Satan is out of it and Jesus is back in it, indeed, what it could have been all along, had it not been polluted by sin.

At a deeper level, the millennium will affirm that this is God's world, that he made it for his Son and that it will all be in his hands again. The creation is basically good and the earth must not be written off as 'beyond redemption'. History must end with a consummation rather than a catastrophe, with redemption rather than ruin.

If it is asked why this climax should occur on the 'old' earth before the 'new' earth appears it can be pointed out that the 'world' (i.e. the unbelieving people on the earth) would otherwise never see the victory of good over evil.

And there is a remarkable parallel between our own redemption and that of our planet. In both cases the spiritual regeneration precedes the physical. We have to work out our salvation while still in the 'old' material body until it is 'transformed' into the 'new' one (Phil 3:21). This will mark the completion of the restoration to our original state. In much the same way, the new earth will mark the conclusion of the process begun during the millennium.

The negative aspect is a little more puzzling. Why is Satan

released again at the end of this 'ideal' regime? One can only conclude that it is a convincing demonstration that conditions do not change the human heart. The big lie that sin is environmentally caused is finally exposed. After a thousand years of peace and prosperity, there are still ungrateful and discontented people around.

Of course it needs to be remembered that the millennial rule will not be democratic, but a 'benevolent dictatorship', not chosen by popular vote but imposed by divine choice. It is in this sense that both Christ and Christians will rule with a 'rod [or sceptre] of iron' (2:27; 12:5; 19:15). This is not a symbol of cruel tyranny, as might be supposed, but of strong rule that cannot be broken. It will include strict censorship, for example, which is always resented by the unrighteous.

In spite of the many benefits of this 'good' government, its impartial administration of perfect justice and its generous welfare of all, there will still be many subjects who would rather forfeit these to regain their moral, or rather immoral, autonomy. Their resentful, rebellious hearts will want to be free from the restraints imposed by the Lord and his people. This is why Satan can gather a worldwide force. He can only deceive those who desire what he offers.

It becomes apparent that the millennium is a fitting prelude to the day of judgement. The issue is made crystal clear – to accept or reject the divine rule, the kingdom of heaven on earth. This has been the issue all through history, but in the millennium it comes to a head. This provides the double proof of the need for an eternal separation within the human race. The new universe God intends to create can only be inhabited by those who have voluntarily and eagerly 'entered the kingdom', embracing the will of God for his creatures with glad and thankful hearts.

It is therefore entirely appropriate that the millennial

passage (20:1–10) is immediately followed by that separation on the great day of judgement, for which 'the rest of the
dead', even those lost at sea, 'come to life' again. For them
the 'books' which contain the record of their godless lives
on earth are sufficient evidence for their sentence. The 'book
of life' contains the names of all who remained faithful to
Jesus (3:5), who had part in the first resurrection and
reigned with him for the thousand years.

CHAPTER THREE

The Broader Context

Our study so far has led to the 'pre-millennial' understanding of Revelation 20. That is, the second coming of Christ *pre*-cedes his thousand-year reign on earth, which in turn comes before the final judgement.

But this interpretation is far from universally held in the Christian church. It has been frequently attacked on 'biblical' and 'philosophical' grounds. We shall begin with the former, since divine revelation is more weighty than human speculation.

It is frequently pointed out that this chapter is the *only* passage in the whole Bible that speaks clearly about a 'millennium'. Some go further and would not admit that it is clear even here, since Revelation is 'highly symbolic' and therefore obscure throughout! For either reason or both, it is considered unreasonable to build a major doctrine on these verses.

Hopefully, the preceding exegesis shows that the passage is far from enigmatic when allowed to speak for itself without prior imposed conclusions. And even if it were the only reference, it is still part of the word of God. Once should be enough for God to say what he wants us to hear (and we need to remember the emphatic sixfold repetition of the 'thousand years').

Furthermore, the church has not shown any reluctance to build other teaching on one passage, even one verse! One thinks of the insistence on a trinitarian formula for baptism (based on Matt 28:19; all other references are in the name of Jesus Christ only). Then there is the application of the name 'Israel' to the church (based on one ambiguous phrase in Gal 6:16; over seventy other references in the New Testament all refer to the Jewish people). It would seem that prejudice may be operating when it comes to the millennium!

But there can be genuine 'biblical' objections to building beliefs on one passage, two in particular:

   i.   Negatively, the absence of confirmation
   ii. Positively, the presence of contradiction

Quite simply, if no other scriptures point in the same direction or if many other scriptures point in a different direction, a passage must be re-examined in this light. The latter is the more serious difficulty.

ABSENCE OF CONFIRMATION

Certainly, there is no other unequivocal statement about the millennium elsewhere in the New Testament. But there are a number of indirect references, perhaps all the more impressive because they are incidental.

There are, of course, some clear promises in the rest of the book of Revelation. 'Overcomers' will 'rule the nations' (2:26–27). The redeemed will 'reign on the earth' (5:10). The 'kingdom of the world' will become the 'kingdom of Christ' (11:15). Chapter 20 is clearly the fulfilment of these predictions.

When we turn to Paul's letters we find a number of hints. Perhaps the clearest is in his first letter to Corinth. Upbraiding the Corinthian believers for suing each other in pagan courts, he says: 'Do you not know that the saints will judge the world? And if you are to judge the world, are you not competent to judge trivial cases?' (1 Cor 6:3). This cannot refer to the final judgement, which is in the hands of the Lord alone. It points to a day when Christians will be responsible for the administration of justice. Note that Paul assumes they have already been told about this.

Later, in the same letter, dealing with the subject of resurrection, he describes the order in which people will be raised, apparently in three phases:

i.   'Christ, the *first* fruits;
ii.   *then*, when he comes, those who belong to him.
iii. *Then* the end will come' (1 Cor 15:23–24).

Admittedly, the third phrase does not mention resurrection specifically. Nevertheless, he does not state that there will be a 'general' resurrection of the whole human race at the time of Christ's return. But the two Greek words translated 'then' (*epeita* and *eita*) both mean 'subsequent'; if the third event was 'concurrent' with the second, another word would have been used (*tote*). He immediately proceeds to talk about a 'reign' of Christ *preceding* 'the end' which culminates in the final vanquishing of death itself (1 Cor 15:25–26; cf. Rev 20:14).

That Paul believed in a resurrection of faithful Christians *before* the rest of mankind is confirmed by his use of a most unusual phrase (in Phil 3:11). Normally translated: 'resurrection from the dead', the Greek phrase actually includes a double preposition, *ek*, literally: 'the *out*-resurrection *out* from the dead', which may be paraphrased: 'out from among the dead'. In other words, this is not a general resurrection of all, but of a limited event predating that.

Not surprisingly, it is used of Jesus himself (e.g. 1 Pet 1:3). Here, Paul is using it of Christians who 'press on' to '*attain*' it. Nothing needs to be done to attain the general resurrection (except to die!). Clearly, Paul is referring to the 'first resurrection' of the 'blessed and holy' (Rev 20:6).

In the same letter Paul looks forward to the day when 'at the name of Jesus every knee will bow . . . and every tongue confess that Jesus Christ is Lord' (Phil 2:10–11; cf. Isa 45:23 and Rev 5:13). When did he expect this universal recognition to take place?

Writing to Timothy, and perhaps quoting an early hymn, Paul promises: 'If we endure, we will also reign with him' (2 Tim 2:12; cf. Rev 3:21). This saying is a perfect summary of the whole message of Revelation. Note that almost all the New Testament references to Christians reigning are in the *future* tense (Rom 5:17 is one of the few exceptions; the primary reference here is reigning over sin rather than over others). Followers of Jesus must walk in his footsteps – suffering leads to glory, the cross comes before the crown.

These Pauline references may be few, but that is no excuse for dismissing them. He only mentions the Lord's Supper in one letter, and only then because of its abuse – yet his teaching on that is taken seriously. And his asides are significant precisely because they indicate what he takes for granted.

Working back through the New Testament we come to the book of Acts. We note the same unusual phrase: 'out from among the dead' in the apostolic preaching of Jesus' resurrection (Acts 4:2).

But the crucial reference is right at the beginning, the very last question asked by the disciples before Jesus returned to heaven: 'Lord, are you at this time going to restore the kingdom to Israel?' (Acts 1:6). All scholars agree that by 'kingdom' they meant political autonomy under a monarch of the Davidic dynasty. The question contains four 'premises' (prior assumptions):

i. Israel once had this 'kingdom'.
ii. Israel has lost this 'kingdom'.
iii. Israel will recover this 'kingdom'.
iv. Jesus is the one to achieve this.

The only uncertainty they have is about the timing: now or later?

It is vital to notice that Jesus does not question the question as he often did when they were based on wrong assumptions (a modern example is the trick question: 'Have you stopped beating your wife?'). He accepts all four basic premises and deals only with the query about timing: 'It is not for you to know the times or dates the Father has set by his own authority' (Acts 1:7). In other words, this event will happen. It is already on God's calendar. But the dating is not their concern. There is other immediate business to attend to: to be his witnesses to the ends of the earth by the power of the Holy Spirit (Acts 1:8). That this is the thrust of Jesus' reply will become obvious by imagining another question: 'Lord, are you at this time going to assassinate Pilate and Herod?' Consider the implications if the reply is still: 'It is not for you to know the times or dates the Father has set'. What would the disciples have understood this to mean?

And there is a later indication that this was the conviction the apostles themselves came to in answer to their own question. In his second public sermon, Peter says that Jesus 'must remain in heaven until the *time* comes for God to *restore* everything' (Acts 3:21); the italicised words are exactly the same unusual Greek words as in Acts 1:6. It is hard to resist the conclusion that the apostles had put two and two together after the ascension and realised that the kingdom would be restored to Israel at his return, even though they still did not 'know the time or dates the Father has set' (Acts 1:7).

So Jesus is accepting their belief that one day the monarchy would be restored to Israel. But when can a descendant of David again sit on a throne in Jerusalem? And who will it be? If the answer is not Christ's millennial rule on earth, the New Testament gives no other possibility.

Turning to the Gospels, especially Matthew and Luke, we find the same sort of clues scattered throughout their pages. At the beginning of the story, an angel promises Mary that the Lord God will give her son 'the throne of his father David' (Luke 1:32). This was an earthly throne, not one in heaven, as Mary would have understood.

Jesus was born 'king of the Jews' (Matt 2:2) and he died as 'king of the Jews' (Luke 23:38). The placard of his crime, pinned to the cross on which he was executed, elicited the plea of a dying criminal: 'Jesus, remember me when you come into your kingdom' (Luke 23:42). In spite of all appearances and circumstances, he believed Jesus was the Messiah and would return one day to claim the throne of Israel. Jesus told him that long before then, even that very day, they would be together 'in paradise' (Luke 23:43; note that Jesus avoided the word 'kingdom' and used instead the Persian word for a palace garden, that is, to be in a privileged place with a royal personage).

Others had anticipated this coming monarchy. The ambitious mother of James and John requested that 'one of these two sons of mine may sit at your right hand and the other at your left in your kingdom' (Matt 20:21). Undoubtedly, she saw this 'kingdom' in earthly terms, a restored monarchy in Israel requiring prime and deputy ministers.

Jesus accepts these assumptions but points out that he will not be responsible for the appointments. Again, the Father decides these things (Matt 20:23, note that the places are prepared for the people, not vice-versa).

Jesus did promise the disciples that 'when the Son of Man sits on his glorious throne, you who have followed me will also sit on twelve thrones, judging the twelve tribes of Israel' (Matt 19:28). Some place must be found in our thinking for the fulfilment of this, as well as for more general predictions like 'the meek will inherit the earth' (Matt 5:5). When will this happen?

On a number of occasions, Jesus offered earthly rewards for faithful service. He offered 'riches' and 'property of your own' to those who handled money and other people's possessions with integrity (Luke 16:11–12). In the parables about his return, reliable servants are awarded greater responsibility: to be put in charge of many things (Matt 24:21,23) or of five and ten cities (Luke 19:17). The councils, as well as the courts (1 Cor 6:2), will be in Christian hands.

That Jesus himself believed in two resurrections, separated in time, is indicated by his use of the common term: 'the resurrection of the righteous' (Luke 14:14) and his endorsement of moral qualifications for the first: 'those who are considered worthy of taking part in that age and in the resurrection from [literally, 'out from'] the dead' (Luke 20:35).

So far we have only been skipping through the pages of the New Testament. But the apostles' expectations of the future have their roots in the prophecies of the Old Testament, to which we now turn.

There are, of course, many promises of an earth transformed under the rule of God himself, a time of unparalleled peace and prosperity in which nations can safely engage in multilateral disarmament. Harmony will be matched by longevity in human life. This vision of an earth restored to its original condition pervades the prophets, but is particularly clear in Isaiah.

There are, however, two ambiguities in this Hebrew hope. First, would it be brought about by a divine agent (God himself) or a human one (the Messiah)? Second, could it be done on this old earth or would it require the creation of a new one? This double tension is not resolved within the canon of Jewish scriptures, but by the time of Jesus a programme may be found in other writings (intertestamental literature known today as the 'apocrypha' and 'pseudepigrapha'). An emerging expectation anticipates a Messianic age on the old earth (estimates of its duration vary from forty to one thousand years) *before* God creates a new earth (Isa 65:17). This pattern is remarkably parallel to that outlined in Revelation 20.

There is one scripture which emphatically predicts a time when God's people will rule this world. Significantly, it belongs to the same 'apocalyptic' genre of literature as Revelation, namely, the second half of the book of Daniel. The two writings have a great deal in common and illuminate each other.

In particular, the seventh chapter is quite specific about a future reign of God's people on this earth, especially in verses 13–22. This section begins with 'one like a son of man, coming with the clouds' (verse 13), quoted by Jesus of himself (Mark 14:62) and clearly a reference to his second advent. This is followed by: 'he was given authority, glory and sovereign power; all peoples, nations and men of every language worshipped him' (verse 14). There follow three affirmations that he will share his authority with his people: 'the saints of the Most High will receive the kingdom' (verse 18); 'the Ancient of Days came and pronounced judgement in favour of the saints of the Most High, and the time came when they possessed the kingdom' (verse 22); 'then the sovereignty, power and greatness of the kingdoms *under the whole heaven* will be handed over to the saints, the people of the Most High' (verse 27). The kingdoms thus transferred are specifically defined as 'rising from the *earth*' (verse 17).

It is almost impossible to avoid linking Daniel with Revelation. The parallels are too many to be coincidental and extend even to such details as hair colour (Dan 7:9 and Rev 1:14). The overall picture of the Ancient of Days, Son of Man and the saints taking over the kingdoms on earth in Daniel surely corresponds to the millennium in Revelation.

In summarising this part of our study, it seems right to say that there is considerable evidence, both direct and indirect, that other scriptures confirm the concept of a millennial reign on earth. But what about those that seem to contradict such a notion?

PRESENCE OF CONTRADICTION

It is claimed that some texts actually preclude the possibility that Jesus will ever reign over an earthly kingdom.

There is his much-quoted statement at his trial before Pontius Pilate: 'My kingdom is not of this world' (John 18:36). The little word 'of' has been given many different meanings – not in this world, not like this world, not for this world, etc. However, the statement is more likely to concern the origin and source of his kingdom than its nature and location. Indeed, he went on to say: 'my kingdom is *from* another place'. But there is a practical aspect, namely the power with which it is established and protected, which will

not be by military might. Significantly, in Revelation 19 and
20, when armies gather in the Middle East to attack and
destroy God's people, the latter are not armed to defend
themselves; Christ's word and God's fire achieve the victory
on both occasions.

But the main claim for contradiction of the millennium
rests on those texts which speak of events as *simultaneous*
which would be widely separated in time by a millennial
interlude.

For example, there are verses that appear to speak of a
'general' resurrection of all humankind, righteous and
wicked, at the same time. The words of Jesus spring to
mind: 'A time is coming when *all* who are in their graves will
hear his voice and come out, those who have done good will
rise to live, and those who have done evil will rise to be
condemned' (John 5:29; but note that in verse 25 there is an
earlier selective raising that anticipates this).

There are also verses which imply that the second advent
and the final judgement occur together. '*When* the Son of
Man comes in his glory, and all the angels with him . . . he
will separate the people' (Matt 25:31–32). 'This [God's
vengeance against persecutors] will happen *when* the Lord
Jesus is revealed from heaven in blazing fire with his power-
ful angels' (1 Thess 1:7).

And there are passages which imply that the dissolution
of the old heaven and earth and the creation of the new
heaven and earth follow straight on from his coming (2 Pet
3:3–10). Actually, second century expositors widely used
verse 8 as a proof-text for the millennium, since its mention
of 'a thousand years' came *between* the discussion of his
coming and the announcement of the new creation (see page
72)! Such exegesis sounds somewhat bizarre today, since
that verse is a general statement that could be applied to any
period in history, but its widespread use in this way bears

testimony to the early belief in a millennial rule of Christ after his return.

In all these cases we may have an example of a common feature of prophecy – the foreshortening of separate future events into one prediction. The phenomenon is often illustrated by viewing distant mountains through a telescope, so that separate peaks are apparently linked. The outstanding example in the Old Testament is that only one coming of the Christ is seen, whereas later revelation shows that there will be two advents, widely separated in time. There is a specific case in Isaiah (65:17–25), which blends in one vision the millennium on the old earth and eternity in the new; people will die at a much greater age in the former, but not at all in the latter.

There are examples in Jesus' predictions as well. A simple one is his compression of the intermediate state of Hades with the ultimate state of hell in the parable of the rich man and Lazarus (Luke 16:19–26). A more complex case is his condensing of the fall of Jerusalem in AD 70 and the disasters preceding his return into one discourse, so that it becomes quite difficult to know to which he is referring (Matt 24; Mark 13; Luke 21).

Jesus did not need to give full details whenever he mentioned the future. That would have involved needless repetition and could have caused distraction. On each occasion he selected those aspects relevant to the point he was making, if necessary compacting separate items into one statement.

The same may be said of the phrase: 'day of the Lord'. This is used of both the second advent and the last judgement, but to insist that the two events must therefore take place within the same twenty-four hours is to miss the varied meanings of the word 'day', which can equally well refer to an epoch (as in 'the day of the horse and cart is over'). In the Bible 'the day of the Lord' is in contrast to the era when sin and Satan have been allowed to govern the world. It is the 'day' when the Lord directly intervenes in world affairs, to bring his purposes to completion. The 'length' of that 'day' is immaterial.

CHAPTER FOUR

The Philosophic Problem

Intellectual difficulties prevent some from embracing the idea of a future, earthly millennium. They simply cannot comprehend how such a state of affairs could be brought into being or maintained. The problem may simply be a lack of imagination, unable to envisage such a radical change in our social and natural environment.

Others find it hard to fit it all together. The most common riddle is how resurrected saints with new bodies can live alongside mortals still in their 'first' mode of existence – overlooking the fact that this precise situation has already occurred between Jesus' resurrection and ascension. He sat and talked with his disciples, ate with them, even cooked breakfast for them.

But mortals will still have sexual appetites and activity, while the risen saints 'neither marry nor are given in marriage' (Luke 20:35). How will they feel about this? Will they be above temptation?

Then there are questions about location and communication. If Jesus is reigning bodily he can only be in one place at a time. Will he stay in Jerusalem or travel? And how can his scattered deputies governing different regions be said to be 'with the Lord for ever' after his second coming (1 Thess 4:17)?

It is quite easy to compile a huge list of such perplexing questions. But it would be highly improbable if we get any answers beforehand. The fact is that the Bible does not deal with such matters. One of the most striking features of Revelation 20 is its total silence about conditions during the 'thousand years'. Clearly, it would not help us to know any more than we do. Indeed, such speculative meditation could prove a dangerous distraction from the vital task of living this present decisive phase of our existence.

We also need to remember that it is just as hard, if not harder, to imagine what endless life on the new earth will be like. We would have had real problems picturing life in this world if we could have been told about it before we were born. Even our forefathers would have found it well-nigh impossible to picture men driving a car and playing golf on the moon, using televisions and computers, engineering genes. The important point is that our comprehension is limited by our present knowledge and experience and it is very foolish to say a thing is impossible simply because we don't understand how it could work.

However, we need to identify the reasons why we find it difficult to believe some things. Behind many of the practical questions already mentioned there lurks a major mental blockage due to the Greek influence on Western philosophy.

The millennium is essentially a Hebrew concept and therefore alien to Greek thought. Linked as it is to the hope of *bodily* resurrection, itself an object of ridicule to those who believed in the immortal soul needing to be set free from its physical prison (cf. Acts 17:32), the whole idea of a future period of existence in this material world is offensive.

For the Greeks never managed to get the spiritual and physical realities properly related. Unlike the Hebrews, whose doctrine of creation prevented them from segregating the two spheres, the Greek thinkers sharply distinguished between eternal and temporal, sacred and secular, heaven and earth, soul and body. Plato concentrated on the former and Aristotle on the latter; neither 'got it together'.

This led to an ambiguous attitude to the 'flesh', leading to extremes of indulgence or repression. Inevitably 'evil' came to be associated and even identified with the physical aspect of existence. Consequently 'salvation' was the liberation of the 'soul' from the body and its environment, either through discipline or death.

Nothing could be further from biblical truth, which affirms that the physical universe is basically 'good' (Gen 1), spoiled only by moral pollution. Physical appetites, including sex, were intended by God to be enjoyed. The body can be a holy temple, a dwelling-place for God's Spirit. His eternal purpose includes immortal bodies in a renewed universe.

Even in the days of the New Testament, the battle was 'joined' between these utterly different philosophies (see 1 Tim 4:1–5 for just one example). The insidious influence of such 'Gnosticism' (the claim to superior knowledge of reality, the opposite of 'agnosticism') became a major threat to the Judeo-Christian faith in the second century. Believers were in danger of becoming 'super-spiritual'.

The sad fact is that Greek philosophy took over the major part of the Christian church and has coloured, or rather discoloured, theology to this very day. Scripture is read through Greek spectacles by most Westerners (it is vital to realise that though the New Testament is written in the common, *koine*, Greek of its day, all but one of its writers and all of its thought were Hebrew).

This disaster happened in North Africa. Alexandria, on the Egyptian coast, boasted the most prestigious university in the ancient world after Athens. Being outside Greece, its unique contribution was to apply Greek philosophy to other cultures. It was here that the Old Testament was translated into the Greek language by seventy scholars, it is said (hence its name, the 'Septuagint' or 'LXX' for short). But with language can come thought and Jewish scholars began to 'think Greek', the most notable being Philo.

Much later, the same subtle process affected Christian theologians in this university, notably Clement and Origen. The latter developed a radically new method of handling scripture: the *allegorical*. He taught his students to look behind the literal statements in the Bible and find the 'spiritual' meaning and message. This was a major step away from the 'plain sense' and has persisted to the present ('You don't still take the Bible literally, do you?'). Its modern form treats scripture as a source of 'values' rather than facts.

This 'spiritualising' method was taken much further by a bishop in Hippo (now in Tunisia), called Augustine. His promiscuous youth left him with a strong association of 'physical' and 'evil'; for ever after he regarded all sexual activity as morally compromised, even within marriage. It is perhaps understandable that he wholeheartedly embraced Plato's detachment of the 'spiritual' from the material which he had thoroughly studied in his 'classical' education. But it was a disaster for the church when he recast Christian doctrine within this framework. More than any other, he has influenced subsequent thinking, both Catholic and Protestant. It is no exaggeration to say that he succeeded in changing the church's mind-set from Hebrew to Greek.

While this has affected many major doctrines, we are concerned with its influence on millennialism. As we shall see, the only view of which we have any record in the 'church fathers' (as the scholars of the first few centuries are called) is the 'pre-millennial' interpretation of Revelation 20 already expounded – that is, the bodily return of Jesus will lead to his reigning on earth, for a thousand years before the day of judgement. There is no trace of any discussion or difference up to the time of Augustine.

But he changed all that. There is evidence that in his earlier ministry he believed and taught what had up till then been the 'orthodox' pre-millennial position, apparently universally held without question. But this understanding is incompatible with Platonic philosophy. It is far too physical to be spiritual, far too earthy for the 'kingdom of heaven'. Radical adjustments would have to be made, two in particular.

The first was to break the sequence in Revelation, separating 'chapter 20' from 'chapter 19' so that the order could be reversed and the 'millennium' passage then claimed to be a 'recapitulation' of events preceding the second advent, rather than following it. It is said to be a description of the 'church age' (which by then had only been five hundred years; now, fifteen centuries later, the figure of 'a thousand' must be regarded as a 'symbol' for at least two thousand!).

This change planted the seeds of the *post*-millennial view – the belief that Jesus will return *after* (i.e. 'post') the millennium. But that raised another question: after what kind of a 'millennium'? Even in Augustine's day, after the Emperor Constantine's conversion and the establishment of Christianity as the only recognised state religion, it was still somewhat difficult to see the world as totally under the control of Christ. More especially, the evidence hardly showed that Satan was no longer at work in it. So another major shift in interpretation was made.

This second move made the millennium a 'spiritual' reign. Christ rules in heaven rather than on earth, though this rule is manifested on earth wherever the gospel is preached and the church established. It is only within this sphere (the 'City of God', as Augustine called it) that Satan can be bound and banished.

This change planted the seeds of the 'a-millennial' view – that Christ will never rule on earth in the 'earthly' sense (as in the 'throne of David'). The pre-fix 'a-' really means 'non-' (as in 'a-theist') but there is widespread reluctance to use the term 'non-millennial' to describe this position, since that would seem to imply a rejection of Revelation 20. The careful reader may have already realised that most 'a-millennialism' is really a 'spiritual' form of 'post-millennialism', and we shall be treating it as such.

Augustine carried so much weight that the pre-millennialism of the first few centuries was actually condemned as heresy by the Council of Ephesus in AD 431! It has been widely suspected ever since, by Catholic and Protestant alike, though the last two centuries have seen a rekindled interest, not least because of a renewed longing for the return of the Lord, stimulated by the deteriorating state of the world, which few would now deny.

This historical/philosophical background is a necessary preliminary to looking at the range of attitudes today. The three main positions were all in place by the sixth century. The 'pre-millennial' early church had become the 'post-millennial' or 'a-millennial' later church, through the Augustinian influx of Platonic philosophy.

But time has not stood still. Nor has thought. There have been developments in all three positions:

Some post-millennialists have returned to the concept of an earthly, political reign of Christ, through a church which will take over world government for an extended period *before* he returns. We must therefore distinguish between 'spiritual' and 'political' post-millennialism.

Pre-millennialism reappeared early in the nineteenth century, but in a new guise. It was part of a novel theological framework which divided the history of the world into seven distinct epochs, called 'dispensations', in each of which God dealt with mankind on a very different basis, or 'covenant'. The final 'dispensation' will be the restored 'kingdom' of Israel ruled over by Christ in Jerusalem, while Christians remain in heaven. So we must now distinguish between 'dispensational' pre-millennialism of modern times and its 'classical' form in the early church.

True 'a-millennialism', in its proper sense of 'non-millennialism', is really the product of the widespread 'liberalism' in the twentieth century. This either rejects the whole idea of a Christian 'millennium' as absurd, dismissing Revelation 20 altogether; or it regards the chapter as a 'myth'; a non-historic fable containing insights but not foresight (the 'thousand years' is simply part of the 'poetic' framework, like the 'six days' in the creation 'myth' and does not refer to any particular period of time). We will refer to these as 'sceptical' and 'mythical' forms of 'a-millennialism'.

Though there are some minor variations within them, this sixfold classification is the best we can come up with for contemporary discernment and discussion. The reader who has already given the matter some thought may identify his or her position by working through the eliminating questionnaire below.

1. Do you believe that the phrase 'a thousand years' in Revelation 20 refers to a particular period of earthly history?
   NO: you are an A-MILLENNIALIST; proceed to 2.
   YES: proceed to 3.
2. Does the passage have any meaning for us today?
   NO: you are a SCEPTICAL A-MILLENNIALIST.
   YES: you are a MYTHICAL A-MILLENNIALIST.

3. Will Christ return after or before the thousand-year period?

   AFTER: you are a POST-MILLENNIALIST; proceed to 4.

   BEFORE: you are a PRE-MILLENNIALIST; proceed to 5.

4. Does the 'thousand years' symbolically cover the whole of church history from first to second advent or literally the final part?

   WHOLE: you are a SPIRITUAL POST-MILLENNIALIST.

   PART: you are a POLITICAL POST-MILLENNIALIST.

5. Will the 'thousand year' period be essentially Christian or Jewish in character?

   CHRISTIAN: you are a CLASSICAL PRE-MILLENNIALIST.

   JEWISH: you are a DISPENSATIONAL PRE-MILLENNIALIST.

So now you know! Or do you? If you are still in doubt, read on. Hopefully all will become clear as we examine each of these six positions in detail. We shall look at each from three perspectives: historical (how, when and why it developed), exegetical (how Revelation 20 is handled) and practical (its implications for evangelism and social action).

Of course, it is virtually impossible to be totally objective, especially in the last area, which is based on observation rather than statistics. And the discerning reader will have already guessed this writer's position ('classic pre-millenni-alism', in case you hadn't!). This study will conclude with a personal statement of the reasons for this conviction.

Nevertheless, a sincere attempt will be made to make a fair presentation of the various views. None is without difficulties, but some have rather more than others! Nor is the matter settled by majority vote, which has varied greatly in time and place.

For 'evangelical' readers, one question ought to be uppermost: which 'correctly handles the word of truth' (2 Tim 2:15)?

CHAPTER FIVE

The Different Views

1. 'SCEPTICAL' A-MILLENNIALISM

This view can only arise in the mind of someone who no longer believes in the inspiration and authority of scripture; who says the Bible may 'contain' the Word of God, but does not constitute it. It is a mixture of divine inspiration and human imagination. Discernment is needed to distinguish the wheat from the chaff. What the criteria are for this exercise varies from person to person and is therefore highly subjective. It has been called: 'reading the Bible with a pair of scissors'!

Revelation 20 is usually dismissed, along with most of the book and other 'apocalyptic' portions of scripture, frequently with a certain amount of contempt.

Underlying these sweeping rejections is a rationalistic scepticism born of the Enlightenment, which contaminated theological and biblical studies in Germany towards the end of the nineteenth century. The movement was labelled, 'Higher Criticism' of the Bible (as opposed to 'Lower Criticism' which simply sought to reconstruct the most accurate text). The basic assumption was that the supernatural realm (if it even exists) cannot affect the natural (Platonic dualism again!). Thus, miracles are excluded, unless a 'naturalistic' explanation can be found for them; as is prophecy, when predicting the future. Since Revelation is largely the latter, it is highly suspect and virtually expunged from the Bible. So we are not able to critique the exegesis of this view!

However, it has to be admitted that some evangelicals, while disagreeing violently in principle with this approach, agree with it in practice! Whether consciously or unconsciously, they neglect the 'apocalyptic' scriptures in general and ignore the millennial issue in particular. They do not feel it important to wrestle with the meaning of Revelation 20, regarding the debate over it as an academic distraction of no practical or spiritual value.

This, of course, is to accuse the early church of error when Revelation was included in the 'canon' (= rule of measurement) of scripture. Incredibly, all the major Protestant Reformers (Luther, Calvin and Zwingli) were of this opinion!

The effects of this neglect vary according to how seriously other scriptures are taken. Heirs of the Reformation still hold firmly to the other major features of the end-time: the return of Christ, the day of judgement, hell and heaven. But there is less interest in the earth, both old and 'new'.

In the absence of a real meeting between the kingdom of heaven and the kingdoms of earth in the millennium, evangelicals concentrated on the former and the next world, while liberals concentrated on the latter and this world. Thus was born the 'social gospel', which interpreted 'kingdom' in terms of improved political and cultural conditions here and now; it would be established by human revolution rather than by divine intervention. This concept carries quite a high degree of motivation to be involved in society.

But the result is that there is very little difference between Christian and humanist hopes for the future. The second coming of Christ tends to slide from the centre to the periphery of expectation. It may still be a credal item, but has ceased to be the 'blessed hope' (Tit 2:13), the return of the only person with the ability to put this world to rights.

So there is great emphasis on love, some on faith, but little on hope. Readers should readily recognise this in preaching and practice.

2. 'MYTHICAL' A-MILLENNIALISM

This takes Revelation 20 more seriously, treating it as scripture with a message. Yet at the same time its plain, simple sense as a prediction of future events is rejected, by treating it as fiction rather than fact.

It is important to understand the meaning of the word 'myth' when applied to scripture. It does not mean 'untrue', though its frequent association with 'legend' can give that impression. The word defines the *kind* of truth to be found in it. The 'story' may not report literal events that have happened or will happen but may still contain moral or spiritual 'truths' which correspond to reality. They range from Aesop's fables to Jesus' parables.

One characteristic of such myths is that not all their features are significant for the truth. Some may simply be part of the literary framework, the 'poetic licence' of the writer, to capture and sustain interest. It is the 'essence' of the myth that contains its message. The details must not be pressed too far. They are not total allegories in which everything stands for something.

The first scriptures to be treated as 'myth' were the early chapters of Genesis. This was partly because 'Higher Criticism' could not accept the possibility of 'backwards' prophecy (the divine revelation of the unknown past) any more than 'forwards' (the unknown future); but it was primarily due to the scientific discoveries that contradicted the biblical account. The earth took four and a quarter billion years to reach its present state, rather than six days (a slight discrepancy!). Missing ribs, magic trees and talking serpents were seen as the stuff of fable. Yet the 'myths' contained vital 'truths'. The difficult details were merely literary decoration.

Once started, this resolution of the conflict between science and scripture proved to be a slippery slope. The problem was: where does myth end and history (that is, factual event) begin? Soon the patriarchs Abraham, Isaac and Jacob were suspect; then Moses and the exodus. But the 'stories' were still valued – for 'values', those ideals and standards which govern our lives.

Inevitably, the New Testament came under the same scrutiny. All along, the parables had been understood this way as stories with a message in them. But now events presented as historical and formerly accepted as such came into question. The miracles of Jesus became 'acted parables' and then just parables. The virgin birth 'story' was simply a way of introducing Jesus' unique relationship with his heavenly 'Father' (who then was his earthly father and was he the result of fornication?). The German scholar Rudolf Bultmann took this to the extreme by applying it to the very heart of Christian belief – the bodily resurrection of Jesus – now considered an apostolic fable enshrining the truth that the influence of Jesus survived his passing.

Of course, the book of Revelation seemed ready-made for this 'demythologising' approach. Highly symbolic and full of picture-language, it was an easy target for the mythmakers. It contains insight into the present rather than foresight into the future, existential rather than historical truth. This became known as the 'Idealist' school of interpretation (see pages 101–106 of *When Jesus Returns*).

Mythical truth is timeless and timely; it is applicable anywhere and anytime. So it is unrelated to the passage of time, the flow of history, the order of events. This virtual removal of time reference from Revelation has serious consequences for the interpretation and application of its message, not least for chapter 20.

The 'millennium' is not a particular period of time; the 'thousand years' stands for any or all time. The truth it contains is that Christ and Christians together are able to take over the territory of Satan (assuming that the devil himself is not a myth, a mere personification of evil!).

Undoubtedly this is true and this truth is a great encouragement to believers under pressure, fitting in with the purpose of Revelation. But is it the whole truth contained in this passage? To limit its message to this single theme is to ignore many of the specific details – for example, the 'first' and 'the rest' resurrections and the release of Satan. Above all, it ignores the sequence of events in the series of visions of which this one is only a part.

So, while this interpretation is in one sense 'true', it is far from an adequate explanation. It rules out any real ground for believing that Christ will one day rule this world after Satan is banished from it. In theological terms, the 'eschatological' dimension of the gospel (what will *certainly* happen in the end) is changed into an 'existential' mode (what can *possibly* happen in the present).

'Mythical' is preferable to 'sceptical' a-millennialism, in that it does make something of Revelation, though not much. 'Spiritual' post-millennialism, to which we now turn, makes rather more. The two are not always easy to distinguish, since the difference seems to be one of degree rather than kind. Hence the common confusion around the term 'a-millennial'. This term should be limited to the view that 'the thousand years' has no reference to any particular period of time, whereas 'post-millennial' applies this term to the church age between the first and second advents of Christ, either in whole ('spiritual') or in part ('political').

3. 'SPIRITUAL' POST-MILLENNIALISM

As we have already seen, this is the second oldest viewpoint, appearing in the fourth and fifth centuries, primarily through the teaching of Augustine.

It was partly a reaction against somewhat unwise earlier preaching about the physical features of the millennial kingdom, which went beyond the scriptural and bordered on the sensual. Augustine said he was induced to forsake the pre-millennial view of the early 'fathers', because some had perverted the doctrine with 'carnal' notions.

However, it was primarily due to his embracing Platonic 'dualism', which distinguished between spiritual and physical, but not clearly between physical and evil ('carnal' covered both). To this thinking, the traditional concept of the millennium seemed far too 'earthy' (later Christians would use the word 'worldly').

So the millennium was transferred from the future to the present (the second advent being 'post' = 'after' rather than 'pre' = 'before' this) and shorn of its physical and political context. It was 'spiritualised', with Christ ruling in heaven and only on earth through his body, the church.

Revelation 20 is taken much more seriously than by true 'a-millennial' interpretation. An explanation is offered for every element. But the major innovation is to treat this chapter as a recapitulation of events leading up to 19, thus breaking the sequence of visions. This radical step involves quite different interpretations.

The 'thousand years' were taken quite literally at first as the length of the church age, but now, after two thousand years, must be seen as a 'symbolic' pointer to an extended period, since the 'millennium' is considered to cover the whole age between the two advents.

Since it is obvious that Satan still has considerable influence in the world, his banishment is reduced to his 'binding', which only limits his 'imprisonment' to preventing the spread of the gospel. The 'angel' who bound him was Christ (Matt 12:29).

The martyrs are reigning with Christ in heaven; this began at the moment of death when they went to be with the Lord. The first resurrection cannot now be understood as a bodily event; it must refer to regeneration, that conversion experience in which we are 'raised' with Christ (Eph 2:6). It is not, therefore, corporate but a separate event for each individual.

The 'coming to life' for 'the rest' is a corporate and physical event, the 'general' resurrection of righteous and wicked at the second advent for the day of judgement. This means, of course, that all those who experience the 'first' resurrection (i.e. conversion) will also be included in the second. They will 'come to life' twice. This makes nonsense of 'the rest', since it now includes everybody!

The 'release of Satan' for the final fling will take place just before the second advent and refers to the battle of Armageddon. Thus Revelation 19:19–21 and 20:7–10 are parallel accounts of the same conflict, the destructive force being both the word of Christ (19:15) and the fire from heaven (20:9).

The reader must judge whether this is genuine *ex*egesis (bringing out of the text what is already there) or manipulated *eis*egesis (putting into it what is not already there). To put it simply, is the text being interpreted in line with a preconceived scheme? Is it being 'forced to fit' a predetermined pattern?

What is clear is that a number of the statements (e.g. 'the first resurrection') are taken metaphorically rather than literally, hence the superficial similarity with 'mythical' a-millennialism. Even more striking is the arbitrary switching from metaphorical to literal with the same phrase in the same context ('come to life').

Nevertheless, this line of interpretation has been the most widely accepted in the church through the ages. What has been the effect on Christian hope?

The answer is: pessimism about this world and optimism about the next. The world is expected to remain much the same. As the population increases, both the kingdom of God and the kingdom of Satan will expand. The wheat and tares will 'both grow together' until the time of the harvest (Matt 13:30). Indeed, just before the end, the situation will get worse, with the 'release' of the sower of tares.

The hopes of a whole world brought back under the rule of God are postponed until the 'new earth' appears, ushered in immediately after the second advent, when the judgement takes place. Then, and only then, will the kingdom have truly and fully come 'on earth as it is in heaven' (though there is a noticeable lack of emphasis on the 'new *earth*' among advocates of this position).

This whole scheme appears to offer a satisfying explanation of the present state of the world, combined with a stimulating expectation for the future. The latter provides quite a strong motive for evangelism but the belief that this world is unlikely to get much better tends to inhibit social action. The underlying Platonic dualism tends to emphasise 'saving souls' rather than bodies at the individual level (consistently, Augustine taught the cessation of healing miracles after the 'apostolic' age; he was forced to revise his opinion towards the end of his ministry when such things began to happen in his own church!).

Ironically, a much more optimistic version of post-millennialism also claims Augustine as its father. There was an ambiguity in his thinking about this world, wavering between pessimism and optimism about the church's influence upon it. We shall now look at the more hopeful version.

4. 'POLITICAL' POST-MILLENNIALISM

At the time of Augustine, two political developments had taken place which radically affected Christian thinking about the future. On the one hand, the Roman Empire had become 'Christian'. The 'conversion' of Constantine (at the battle of the Milvian bridge north of Rome, when he had seen the logo of Christ in the sky and heard a voice saying: 'In this sign, conquer') had led to the 'establishment' of Christianity as the imperial religion and later to the suppression of other religions (including Judaism). The church had conquered the world, though the discerning wondered if it wasn't the other way round as they saw the world come into the church in more ways than one! It was the birth of 'Christendom', as it was later to be known, an earthly 'kingdom of Christ' – ruling through his vicarious (= delegated) people and subsequently his 'vicar', the papa (= father) or pope of his people. Conquering Rome in the name of Christ seemed a harbinger for the 'conversion' of the whole world.

On the other hand, the empire itself was under attack on its borders, notably by 'barbarians' from the north. Rome would be sacked and the Emperor would move east to the new capital of Constantinople. All this did nothing to discourage Augustine's belief that the church would survive

such political disasters, that fallen empires would be re-
placed by 'the City of God'. Rome might disappear, but the
church of Rome would take its place (it is interesting to note
that to this day the popes have used the imperial title
'pontifex maximus', insignia of office and even vestments
of the former Emperors).

So the church, or kingdom of Christ, would rise like a
phoenix from the flames of war threatening all political
states. It would survive and grow, despite all apparent
setbacks, for God was with it.

This more confident strand in Augustine's thought inevitably raised the question: will the church, then, reach the
point where Christians will be able to take over the government of the whole world? Over the centuries this hope has
kept coming – and going.

During the great age of exploration, when new continents
were being discovered, Catholic priests, motivated by this
ecclesiastical imperialism, sailed with the explorers. Many
Protestant missionary hymns of the nineteenth century
('Jesus shall reign where'er the sun') reveal the same global
ambition. This view has always been popular when the
church is enjoying a wave of advance.

This outlook has had its setbacks in the twentieth century
(not least two 'world wars' centred in 'Christian' Europe,
which were a contributory factor to the spreading secular-
ism that has followed). Yet, surprisingly, there has been a
recent revival of post-millennial optimism.

This has centred in the Western world with 'Restoration'
movements in Britain and 'Reconstruction' movements in
America. A 'Dominion' theology teaches that the redeemed
are called to rule the earth (Gen 1:28 is by implication
extended to include humans as well as animals) by 'disci-
pling the nations' (Matt 28:19 is taken to refer to political
states rather than various ethnic groups). In a word, the

church is called, even commanded, to 'take over' the world and establish a 'political' kingdom of heaven on earth, thus bringing the 'millennium' into being. Note that this is without Jesus needing to return and therefore before he returns – to find his kingdom all ready for him!

This latest form of post-millennial thinking obviously carries an extremely strong motivation for social action and not much less for evangelism (since the 'take-over' depends to some degree on the proportion of Christians in the population). The world can be 'Christianised' without everyone in it becoming a Christian. The important thing is that the power and authority will need to be in Christian hands. The church 'militant' will become the church 'triumphant', not just in heaven, but here on earth.

How does this outlook handle Revelation 20 (though this is not a primary basis for their case)? Most of it is taken in exactly the same way as the 'spiritual' post-millennialists (see the previous section) with two significant exceptions.

First, the 'thousand years' is taken quite literally as the final millennium of the church age, ten centuries of peace and prosperity under Christian government. It is important to notice that this era has not yet begun.

Second, the millennial rule is wholly on earth and of an earthly kind. It is political. It will be recognised by the whole population, believer and unbeliever alike.

In both these aspects, this form of post-millennialism is much nearer the pre-millennialism of the early church. But the biggest difference remains – it is achieved without the return of Christ and his bodily presence.

And there are some major theological objections to this scenario. For one thing, it tends to confuse 'church' and 'kingdom', which are not identified in the New Testament. The church may be a community, a 'colony', of the kingdom, but it is not the kingdom itself, which extends far beyond the church. When the church thinks of itself as a 'kingdom', its leaders start behaving like kings and build their own little kingdoms. Imperialism replaces evangelism.

More serious, there is a failure to recognise the tension between the 'now' and the 'not yet' of the 'kingdom' in the New Testament. It has come and it has not come. It has been inaugurated but not consummated. Half of Jesus' parables envisage its coming as a gradual process of human infiltration and half as a sudden crisis of divine intervention (the parable of the wheat and tares combines both concepts; Matt 13:24–30, 36–43). The kingdom may be 'entered' now, but it will not be universally 'established' until the king returns.

This failure leads to a comparative neglect of the second coming, which was so central to the apostolic preaching. This event is mentioned over three hundred times in the New Testament and the expectation figures largely in its practical application of belief to behaviour. But in the viewpoint we are considering, this advent fades almost into insignificance. Obviously, if the millennium has to precede the return and has not even started yet, the 'hope of his coming' is too far away to affect us deeply. It belongs to the dim and distant future – whereas previous generations expected him 'soon', hopefully within their lifetime, which profoundly affected their way of living.

Finally, there is one major difficulty – does it look as if the church will soon be governing the world? After two thousand years, is the church any nearer this goal? Some cynics might observe that the church seems incapable of running its own affairs, never mind everyone else's!

Whatever else it is, political post-millennialism is a 'triumph of hope over experience'. Can such high expectations be sustained? The Bible recognises that 'hope deferred makes the heart sick' (Prov 13:12), but we are asking whether the hope is true or false, not just whether it will be soon or late. Has God promised it or not?

Will Revelation 20 be fulfilled before Jesus returns? If so, then most believers may hear of it in heaven or even see it from there (Heb 12:1?), but they will not be part of it. They will never experience it for themselves. It will have come too late.

If it is fulfilled after Jesus returns and the 'first resurrection', all believers will have the joy of living in a world under Christian control. We will now turn our attention to this 'pre-millennial' view.

5. 'CLASSICAL' PRE-MILLENNIALISM

This view takes a middle course between the *pessimism* of 'spiritual' post-millennialism, which believes this world is not likely to get much better, and the *optimism* of 'political' post-millennialism, which believes this world will be 'Christianised' by the church. It can make a fair claim to *realism*, by believing that this world will only recover its original state when Christ is back in it, and Satan is cast out of it.

It takes Revelation 20 in its plain, simple sense (if that is taken to be its 'literal' sense, its exponents plead guilty). The sequence of visions is accepted, placing Christ's millennial rule on earth with his saints, particularly the martyrs, after the second advent and before the day of judgement. The righteous will be raised first at the beginning of the thousand years and the rest at the end. Satan will be totally restricted for the greater part but released for the final denouement. In fact, ask a pre-millennialist what he believes and he might well say: 'Read Revelation 19–20 without listening to anyone else'!

This is probably why this seems to have been the unanimous position of the church for the first few centuries. They simply had the scripture and were not faced with the bewildering variety of interpretations we have to choose from today.

'Classic' means that this was the earliest belief – and the only one for a considerable time. The early fathers believed in 'the corporeal reign of Christ on this very earth' (to quote Papias, bishop of Hierapolis in Asia). Some (for example, Justin Martyr) associated this with the restoration of the kingdom to Israel, though not all were agreed on this. Many other names are cited as holding this 'pre-millennial' position – among them Barnabas, Hermas, Ignatius, Polycarp, Irenaeus, Justin Martyr, Tertullian, Hippolytus, Methodius, Commodian and Lactantius.

There is negative as well as positive evidence from these early centuries. Not a single trace has been found of any alternative view in the many documents that have survived. Michael Green, commenting on the quotation of Psalm 90:4 ('With the Lord a day is like a thousand years, and a thousand years are like a day') in 2 Peter 3:8, says: 'This verse, Ps.xc.4, became, in the second century, the main proof-text of chiliasm, the doctrine that Christ would reign for a thousand years at the parousia. This belief became almost an article of Christian orthodoxy from the time of the writing of Revelation to Irenaeus' (in the Tyndale Commentary 2 *Peter and Jude*, Inter-Varsity Press, 1968 p.34).

Criticism of the prevailing view only surfaced with Clement and Origen (significantly, in the 'Greek' culture of Alexandria). The first direct challenges are associated with Eusebius, Tyconius and Constantine in the fourth century and Augustine in the fifth. The latter's post-millennialism was to become the orthodoxy of the 'Catholic' church, which later condemned the earlier 'chiliasm' as 'heresy'.

However, it never died out. In small groups that studied the Bible for themselves, during the centuries when most simply accepted the traditions of the church, pre-millennialism reappeared – for example, among the Paulicians, Waldenses, Lollards and Wycliffites.

Even when the 'magisterial' Reformers (so-called because they relied on the Constantinian church-state alliance to bring about change) hung on to the Augustinian post-millennialism, pre-millennialism was rediscovered by the radical left wing of the 'Anabaptists'. Alas, a few of these became extremist and gathered in Munster, Germany, to set up the millennial kingdom. Though this fiasco is often cited to discredit chiliasm, it needs to be pointed out that, in practice, this was a fanatical form of political post-millennialism!

Among pre-millennialists of a later age is the eminent scientist, Sir Isaac Newton. In the nineteenth century a surprising number of Anglican bishops held this view (Ryle, Westcott and Lightfoot, for example), though few, if any, would today.

So there has been a continuous witness through the ages, though after Augustine it often dwindled to a small minority. It is currently attracting renewed interest as an alternative to 'dispensationalism' (see below), which is losing credibility. The writings of George Eldon Ladd and Merrill C. Tenney have done much to encourage this. Leading pre-millennialists of our day have included Dr Francis Schaeffer and Dr Carl Henry.

However, it is not yet widely held again, so it is difficult to assess the practical effect on evangelism and social action. In theory this should be beneficial because it offers hope for both this world and the next, avoiding both extremes of pessimism and optimism.

Evangelism becomes worthwhile because of the glorious

future envisaged. The faithful followers of Jesus will share his 'reign' in both the old and the new earth (Rev 20:6 and 22:5). This destiny is available to all who will repent of their sin and believe in the Saviour. The alternative is unspeakably horrible (Rev 20:10, 15; 21:8).

Social action becomes worthwhile precisely because it will ultimately be successful. There will come a day when good will overcome evil, justice will replace injustice, peace replace war, plenty replace poverty, and health replace sickness. If a Communist is prepared to sacrifice all for a classless, crimeless society which he may never live to see (and which we now know no Communist will ever live to see!), how much more will a Christian live and work for a 'millennium' which he is certain to see and in which he will play a part?

There is a further personal incentive. If the responsible positions then will be delegated according to integrity and faithfulness now (as Jesus clearly taught; Matt 25:21–23), what a stimulus to be such right now. If the courts are to be in the hands of Christians who can administer justice fairly (1 Cor 6:2), lawyers and judges can be qualifying now. The millennium will need honest bankers, caring councillors and a host of loving men and women to provide truly 'civil' service. In this perspective a whole host of 'secular' jobs become 'sacred' vocations. Taxi-driving and washing-up are as important to God as saving souls. Worship and work come together again.

Of course, some will argue that if it's all going to come right at the second coming, why bother to try to improve the world now, against such heavy odds? Apart from overlooking the fact that sloth can forfeit the future altogether (Matt 25:26–30), such thinking has missed the very essence of Christian motivation. Those who really do believe in what the second coming will bring will seek to have as much of that as they can beforehand. To take a parallel case, those who 'know that when he appears, we shall be like him, for we shall see him as he is' will seek to purify themselves now, 'just as he is pure' (1 John 3:2–3). Those who expect to inherit a fortune are not content to wait if they know they can have a good part of it immediately!

This world is not written off. Jesus is coming back to reclaim it. The more we can reclaim now in his name, the better that will be for his glory, the good of others and even our own future. We can give ourselves 'fully to the work of the Lord' (which for the believer means daily work just as much as 'church' work) because we know that our 'labour in the Lord is not in vain' (1 Cor 15:58).

But there is another version of pre-millennialism which has exactly the opposite effect. Unfortunately, it is the one with which most today are familiar.

6. 'DISPENSATIONAL' PRE-MILLENNIALISM

This is a relative newcomer, of which there is no trace before 1830. This raises the question as to why, if it is the correct interpretation, no one had seen it in scripture before then.

Revelation 20 is taken in much the same way as the 'classical', but the whole thing is then put into a novel framework, the singular features being:

First, the division of world history into seven 'dispensations', eras in each of which God relates to humans on a different basis. The last of these is the millennium, the only one truly deserving the title 'kingdom', since only then is the earth directly ruled by the Lord.

Second, it is this 'kingdom' which Jesus offered to the Jews at his first advent. On their rejection, it was withdrawn and postponed until the second advent. The church age is therefore a 'parenthesis' in God's purpose, which centres on Israel. Jesus' teachings on the kingdom, including the Sermon on the Mount, are primarily applicable to the millennium rather than the church.

Third, the future destiny of Christians is in heaven (they are God's 'heavenly people'), while the Jews will remain on earth (they are his 'earthly people'). For all eternity, 'never the twain will meet'!

Fourth, the church will be 'snatched away' from the earth before the 'Big Trouble' preceding the second advent. This event is called 'the secret rapture', or simply 'the Rapture' (see the section on this on pages 175–182 of *When Jesus Returns*). It is the next event on God's calendar and could happen at 'any moment', without warning. Christians will therefore be absent during the catastrophic events described in Revelation 4–18, but will return to earth with Christ in chapter 19. Whether they stay around with him after that is somewhat vague. What is clear is that:

Fifth, during the millennium the Old Testament kingdom of Israel will be fully restored. A rebuilt temple will see the revival of the sacrificial system (though it is usually qualified to be a 'memorial' to Christ's sacrifice on the cross, a kind of Jewish 'Eucharist', rather than an atoning ritual).

This whole 'dispensational' scheme significantly altered previous pre-millennial thinking. In particular, the millennium became more Jewish than Christian. In spite of its novelty, it took rapid hold, first in Britain and then in America, where it is probably now the majority view among evangelicals.

It originated with a man called John Nelson Darby, an Anglican curate in Dublin who became the founder of the 'Brethren', sometimes known as 'Plymouth' Brethren after one of the strongest early centres of the movement. Originally aimed at uniting Christians from all denominations in spontaneous worship around the 'breaking of bread' and in serious study of scripture, it soon became a denomination of its own, eventually splitting into many separate groups, some very 'open' to other believers and some very 'exclusive'.

From the first there was a deep interest in biblical prophecy to see what would become of the church in its 'ruined' state, as Darby described it. It was he who embraced and taught the 'dispensational' focus on Israel rather than the church and the 'secret rapture' of believers before the 'Great Tribulation'. His views did not go unchallenged; men like Benjamin Newton, S.P. Tregelles, and George Müller (of Bristol orphanage fame) never accepted them. But his dominant personality prevailed and his method of interpreting scripture became Brethren orthodoxy from which few dared to dissent.

Crossing the Atlantic, he convinced a lawyer, Dr C.I. Scofield, of its rightness. He in his turn produced a Bible with notes, in which he incorporated 'dispensational' comments. This 'Scofield' Bible sold exceptionally well among evangelicals in the United States. The danger was that readers found it difficult to remind themselves of the difference between the inspired word of God and the human commentary, accepting the latter as 'in the Bible'.

Today there are seminaries which teach nothing else (Dallas is the best known; the books of one of its students, Hal Lindsay, are known the world over and have sold by the million). Some missionary organisations will only consider candidates with dispensational convictions.

There is no questioning the enormous influence of this teaching.

On the positive side, it has to be said that it has done more than anything else to restore pre-millennialism to the church. Millions again believe that Christ is coming back to earth to reign over this earth for a thousand years.

But the negative results outweigh the positive. The packaging has polluted the contents. The theological framework in which the millennium is enmeshed is fatally flawed.

The most serious error concerns the 'kingdom'. If political post-millennialists have overemphasised the 'now' dimension and seen it largely in its present manifestation, dispensational pre-millennialists have overemphasised the 'not yet' dimension and seen it as exclusively future. This fails to do justice to the now/not yet dialectic of the New Testament.

This inevitably leads to the sharp separation of Jewish and Christian destinies and an unbalanced emphasis on the Jewishness of the millennium. This is contrary to Jesus' prediction of 'one flock and one shepherd' (John 10:16), Paul's concept of one olive tree into which shall be grafted 'the full number of the Gentiles' and 'Israel as a whole' (Rom 11:17–26) and John's vision of a new Jerusalem descending from heaven to earth and bearing the names of the twelve tribes of Israel and the twelve apostles of Christ (Rev 21:12–14).

The division of history into seven dispensations is highly suspect. At the opposite end of the theological spectrum, 'Reformed Calvinists' lump them all together in '*the* covenant of grace' (a phrase not found in scripture). The biblical position seems to deal with two covenants, old and new, law and grace, Moses and Christ; though the 'new' incorporates the covenants with Abraham and David, while all mankind benefits from the covenant with Noah.

This leads on to another problem. The letter to the Hebrews is at pains to show that the 'old' covenant is 'obsolete and ageing' and 'will soon disappear' (Heb 8:13). This includes the whole sacrificial system in Leviticus, which has been 'done away' by Christ's supreme sacrifice on the cross. Its reappearance during the millennium would be an anachronistic anomaly!

The tragedy of all this is that pre-millennialism has become inextricably bound up with dispensational thinking in so many minds that it is assumed they belong together and that it is impossible to have one without the other. When the faults of dispensationalism are discovered, especially by those brought up under it, the tendency is to discard the whole teaching rather than sort out what is true from what is false. The millennium is rejected as one of the dispensations. The baby is thrown out with the bathwater!

Many who do this don't know what to put in its place and vaguely regard themselves as 'a-millennial' – in the true sense of non-millennial. It is not that they are rejecting Revelation 20 in principle, but in practice it is no longer part of their thinking or preaching. Mostly, they are quite unaware of 'classical' pre-millennialism, the view of the early church (one Bible college principal told this author he'd never heard of it!). When they do hear about it, the reaction is usually one of real relief – that it is possible to be pre-millennial without being dispensational.

There is one more aspect to be considered: the practical effect of dispensational pre-millennialism. Of all the views, this probably produces the highest motivation for evangelism. The imminence of Christ's return ('he could come tonight') prompts an urgency in the saved to save others and in the unsaved to be saved. Perhaps the majority of evangelical missionaries sent out from the United States are impelled by this kind of thinking.

However, zeal does not justify motive. Cults produce enthusiastic missionaries (Mormons and Jehovah's Witnesses are good examples), as did the Pharisees in Jesus' day (Matt 23:15). All motives must be tested by scripture.

But if dispensationalism produces the highest motivation for evangelism, it probably has the lowest for social action.

The combined beliefs of an any-moment 'rapture' and a 'Jewish' millennium sap the desire to try and make this world a better place. The attention is focused on heaven rather than earth. What is the point of getting involved in long-term social betterment when Jesus and a saved Israel will be putting it right? For a fascinating study of the effect of this teaching on political endeavour, see: *Living in the Shadow of the Second Coming: American Premillennialism 1875–1982* by Timothy P. Weber (Zondervan 'Academie', 1983).

While both forms of pre-millennialism stimulate evangelism, there is a sharp contrast between them when it comes to social action. Now that more evangelicals are recovering a balance between the two aspects of 'mission', it is very important to draw attention to this marked difference.

CHAPTER SIX

The Personal Conclusion

Our study of the millennial views is over. Hopefully the reader's thinking has been clarified rather than confused! At least by now it will be realised that the debate has a very practical influence and is not just an academic exercise. Our real convictions on the subject have a quite profound effect on our attitude to life.

I have not hidden my own conclusions, which I arrived at quite independently of others. Brought up in the Methodist Church, I never heard the millennium mentioned, much less discussed, though they did sometimes sing about it, perhaps without realising it; one of my favourite hymns as a boy was: 'Sing we the king who is coming to reign . . .' It was when I began to teach the Bible systematically, as a Royal Air Force chaplain, that I began to consider and then study this question. After reading as much as I could of the very different opinions and checking these against scripture, I became convinced that the early church had been right after all and indicated this in my first book (*Truth to Tell*, Hodder and Stoughton, 1977).

Let me summarise my pilgrimage by listing the reasons for my position as a 'classical' pre-millennialist:

1. It is the most 'natural' interpretation of Revelation 20. I felt that others were forcing this scripture into their own mould, giving artificial, even arbitrary,

meanings to some of its features. It is a fundamental principle in my Bible study to let the passage speak for itself, taking it in its plainest, simplest sense unless there is a clear indication to the contrary.

2. It gives the most logical explanation for the second advent. What can he only do by coming back here? Why should Jesus return to planet earth at all? Certainly not for the final judgement, which takes place after earth has 'fled' (Rev 20:11). So for what? And why do we have to come back here with him (1 Thess 4:14)? If he and we are not going to 'reign' on earth for a considerable time, it is difficult to find another adequate reason for his return, or ours.

3. It puts the most emphasis on the second coming. This is related to the point above. Both a-millennialists and post-millennialists tend to play down the second advent, which does not then have the central place it occupies in the New Testament. The reason is simple. If the only, or even the main, desire for his return is to be with him, this will have already happened for the believer at the moment of death (Phil 1:21).

4. It made sense in itself. I could understand why God would want to vindicate his Son in the eyes of the world and stage a final demonstration of what this world was meant to be like and could be like in the right hands. I could even see why he would add a final revelation of the rebelliousness of sin, even in an ideal environment, before the day of judgement. The phased transition from the old earth to the new matched my own redemption, first in my old body, only much later in the new.

5. It 'earths' our future destiny. Those who deny a future millennium rarely talk or even think about

the new earth. Everything in the future centres in heaven. But heaven is only a waiting-room for believers, until they come back to this earth and later on to the new earth, where Father and Son will dwell with us. Instead of going to heaven to live with them for ever, they come to earth to live with us for ever (Rev 21:2–3), as at the beginning (Gen 3:8). All this gives our planet an eternal significance.

6. It strikes a note of realism. It avoids both the gloomy pessimism of those who think this world will never be much better than it is and the naive optimism, even triumphalism, of those who think the church can dethrone Satan and enthrone Christ by taking over the nations herself. Pre-millennialism avoids both extremes, accepting that the world will get worse before it gets better, but certain that it will get better after it gets worse.

7. It has fewer problems than others! It has been frankly admitted that *all* the views have some difficulties. But classic pre-millennialism has far less than the alternatives, especially when it comes to interpreting Revelation 20. There are still many unanswered questions, but I can live with these. It is the easiest to preach with confidence, because it is the one which the common reader is most likely to find in the appropriate passage.

8. It is what the early church believed. The unanimity of the first few centuries is very impressive. They were not infallible, but they were the nearest generations to the apostles. The absence of any debate is striking, as is the fact that differences only appeared when Christian doctrine was polluted by Greek philosophy.

For these reasons, I am able to pray the daily prayer Jesus gave to his disciples with real meaning and desire – 'your kingdom come . . . on earth as it is in heaven' (Matt 6:10) – as much as it can before the coming of Christ and the rest of it after.

Sing we the King who is coming to reign,
Glory to Jesus, the Lamb that was slain,
Life and salvation His empire shall bring,
Joy to the nations when Jesus is King.

Come let us sing: Praise to our King.
Jesus our King, Jesus our King:
This is our song, who to Jesus belong:
Glory to Jesus, to Jesus our King.

All men shall dwell in His marvellous light,
Races long severed His love shall unite,
Justice and truth from His sceptre shall spring,
Wrong shall be ended when Jesus is King.

All shall be well in His kingdom of peace,
Freedom shall flourish and wisdom increase,
Foe shall be friend when His triumph we sing,
Sword shall be sickle when Jesus is King.

Souls shall be saved from the burden of sin,
Doubt shall not darken His witness within,
Hell hath no terrors, and death hath no sting;
Love is victorious when Jesus is King.

Kingdom of Chirst, for thy coming we pray,
Hasten, O Father, the dawn of the day
When this new song Thy creation shall sing,
Satan is vanquished and Jesus is King.

Charles Silvester Horne

When Jesus Returns

David Pawson

What is known about Christ's second coming
and how can we prepare for it?

Christians everywhere await Christ's return. Will he come
to the whole world or just one place? Soon and suddenly or
after clear signs? What can he achieve by coming back here
and how long will it take?

David Pawson brings clarity and insight to these and
many other vital issues surrounding the bodily return of
Jesus Christ to our world, a subject which will continue to
dominate the Church's agenda as the end of the millennium
approaches. Based on a new approach to the interpretation
of the book of Revelation, the controversial subjects of the
'Rapture' and the 'Millennium' are discussed in detail,
completing this vital resource for our times.

ISBN 0 340 61211 8

The Road to Hell

David Pawson

'Hell is the most offensive and least acceptable of all Christian doctrines. We try to ignore it but it won't go away. We attempt to explain it away but it keeps coming back. Better to face the truth, even if it hurts.'

Most of Christ's teaching on this uncomfortable subject was addressed to his followers, yet it hardly features in contemporary preaching. Challenging the modern alternatives of liberal 'universalism' and evangelical 'annihilationism', David Pawson presents the traditional concept of endless torment as soundly biblical, illustrating his argument with in-depth Scripture studies on controversial passages. Heaven is also a reality, he affirms, but it is hell which is being overlooked.

'I am convinced that the recovery of this neglected truth is vital to the health of Christ's body and essential to the task of completing the evangelisation of all the nations.'

'This book has not been written as a contribution to the controversy nor as another voice in the dispute. It is written with obvious compassion, a high regard for God's Word and a godly jealousy for the character of God.'
From the Foreword by Lynn Green

ISBN 0 340 53964 X

Jesus Baptises in One Holy Spirit

How? When? Why?

David Pawson

For the most part, the Church has been silent about Jesus' role as baptiser in the Spirit, though John declared this to be the principle contribution of his Messianic ministry.

Through exploration of the relevant scriptures of both Old and New Testaments, David Pawson describes eight essential elements in Spirit baptism. He maintains that the sacramental, evangelical and pentecostal streams in Christianity have all failed to do justice to this biblical doctrine. In particular its dual purpose of purity and power, for salvation and service, needs to be recovered if we are to become a truly apostolic church in the twenty-first century.

ISBN 0 340 69398 3

Once Saved, Always Saved?

A Study in Perseverance and Inheritance

David Pawson

The majority evangelical view is that once someone has accepted Christ as Saviour they are guaranteed salvation. But is it safe to assume that once we are saved, we are saved for always?

David Pawson investigates this through biblical evidence, historical figures such as Augustine, Luther and Wesley, and evangelical assumptions about grace and justification, divine sovereignty and human responsibility. He asks whether something more than being born again is required so that our inheritance is not lost. This book helps us decide whether 'once saved, always saved' is real assurance or a misleading assumption. The answer will have profound effects on the way we live and disciple others.

ISBN 0 340 61066 2

Word and Spirit Together

Uniting Charismatics and Evangelicals

David Pawson

For the last quarter of a century, Charismatics and Evangelicals had been moving closer together. Now they seem to be drifting apart again, to the detriment of the two fastest growing streams in Christendom.

With personal experience of both, and a passionate desire to see them united, David Pawson has made a searching study of their remaining differences which he believes can be resolved without compromise.

With a Foreword by Clive Calver, former general secretary of the Evangelical Alliance.

ISBN 0 340 72192 8